USER FRIENDLY CHURCHES

Books by George Barna

*The Barna Report 1992–93: An Annual Survey
of Life-styles, Values and Religious Views*

*The Barna Report, What Americans Believe: An
Annual Survey of Values and Religious Views
in the United States*

*Finding a Church You Can Call Home: The
Complete Guide to Making One of the Most
Significant Decisions in Your Life*

*The Frog in the Kettle: What Christians Need to
Know About Life in the Year 2000*

*Marketing the Church: What They Never
Taught You About Church Growth*

*The Power of Vision: How You Can Capture
and Apply God's Vision for Your Ministry*

*Church Marketing:
Breaking Ground for the Harvest*

WHAT IS A USER FRIENDLY CHURCH? IT IS A church that is in touch with the needs of those it wants to serve. Just as a well-designed computer system enables even computer novices to use it effectively, user friendly churches enable a broad spectrum of people to come to know and serve the living God. None of the successful churches described in this book is interested in being user friendly in the sense of compromising the gospel or the historic faith of the church just to make friends with the age. Each of these churches affirms the gospel of Christ boldly and without apology. But they are equally firm in their intent to *listen* to the audiences they target, and to meet contemporary felt needs as the gospel directs.

GEORGE BARNA

AUTHOR OF *THE FROG IN THE KETTLE*

USER FRIENDLY CHURCHES

WHAT CHRISTIANS NEED TO KNOW ABOUT THE CHURCHES PEOPLE LOVE TO GO TO

- WHY THESE CHURCHES DON'T TAKE THE SAFE ROUTE.
- WHAT THEY'RE DOING—AND NOT DOING.
- WHY THEY'VE SACRIFICED THEIR SACRED COWS.
- WHAT'S ATTRACTING SO MANY PEOPLE.

Published by Regal Books
A Division of Gospel Light
Ventura, California 93006
Printed in U.S.A

Regal Books is a ministry of Gospel Light, an evangelical Christian publisher dedicated to serving the local church. We believe God's vision for Gospel Light is to provide church leaders with biblical, user-friendly materials that will help them evangelize, disciple and minister to children, youth and families.

It is our prayer that this Regal Book will help you discover biblical truth for your own life and help you meet the needs of others. May God richly bless you.

For a free catalog of resources from Regal Books/Gospel Light please contact your Christian supplier or call 1-800-4-GOSPEL.

Scripture quotations used in this book are from the HOLY BIBLE, NEW INTERNATIONAL VERSION. Copyright © 1973, 1978, 1984 International Bible Society. Used by permission of Zondervan Bible Publishers.

Also used is the *NRSV, New Revised Standard Version Bible,* copyright 1989, Division of Christian Education of the National Council of the Churches of Christ in the United States of America.

Library of Congress Cataloging-in-Publication Data

Barna, George.
  User friendly churches : what Christians need to know about the churches people love to go to / George Barna.
       p.   cm.
  ISBN 0-8307-1473-1 (trade paper)
    1. Church growth—United States. 2. United States—Church history—
  20th century. I. Title.
BR526.B367   1991
254—dc20
                                                        90-28625
                                                        CIP

2 3 4 5 6 7 8 9 10 11 12 13 14 / X3 / KP / 99 98 97 96 95 94

Rights for publishing this book in other languages are contracted by Gospel Literature International (GLINT). GLINT also provides technical help for the adaptation, translation and publishing of Bible study resources and books in scores of languages worldwide. For further information, contact GLINT, P.O. Box 4060, Ontario, CA 91761-1003, U.S.A., or the publisher.

CONTENTS

USER
FRIENDLY
CHURCHES

ACKNOWLEDGMENTS

THIS BOOK GREW OUT OF A REPORT I WROTE IN 1990, ENTITLED "Successful Churches: What They Have in Common." Many pastors and church leaders acquired the report and provided feedback and encouragement. Without their positive response, this information would still have the limited distribution of a report. It is my prayer that expanding the content of the report into book form and broadening its exposure will enable the Church to reap a richer harvest in the years ahead.

I must also thank the leaders of the churches described in this report. They were gracious with their time, with information and with their ideas about ministry. Sometimes it was their questions, more than their answers to my questions or the descriptions of their experience, that prompted some of the more valuable explorations that appear in these pages. My prayer for them is that God will bless their investment in this project by facilitating the growth and impact of ministry as a direct result of their willingness to share their experiences through this book.

My friend and colleague in ministry, Greg Roth, has again provided useful insights into this project. Along with Tim Galleher, he has helped me shape this book into a more practical and meaningful work.

As always, I am indebted to the staff with whom I work at the Barna Research Group. Their assistance enables me to take breaks to write the reports and books that share with others the fascinating items that we learn about people, churches and ministry. During this period, our core team has included Cindy Fiori, Vibeke Klocke, Larry Linamen, Keith Lindstrom, Paul Rottler, Ron Sellers and Jim Stipe.

Gospel Light has been a wonderful publisher. Few people have been as encouraging and supportive as Bill Greig III. His understanding of and agreement with our emphasis upon the local church, and with our vision for effective ministry, has meant much to me. The support of Bill Greig, Jr., Barb Fisher, Kyle Duncan, Ron Durham, Sharon Hamilton, Mark Maddox, Gloria Moss, Kim Pitman, Dennis Somers and the numerous other skilled members of the GL family has been a true blessing over the course of our relationship.

The biggest blessing, though, has been the support of my wife, Nancy. She has endured the enthusiasm of my new insights and ideas, the frustration of my attempts to communicate new ideas to closed minds, the tension of trying to complete more work than can be humanly accomplished and the sacrifice of time as I have pursued those avenues of outreach in which I have felt led. Her own sharp instincts and perceptions played a significant role in the shaping of the research behind this book. Meanwhile, her ability to manage the research group during my times of hibernation for reflection, writing, and renewal have been indispensable. Most of all, her wholehearted and selfless support of this ministry and of my life are unspeakable gifts of love. I am a blessed man, indeed.

INTRODUCTION

AS ALWAYS, THERE IS GOOD NEWS AND BAD NEWS.

The bad news is that the vast majority of Christian churches in America are either stagnant or declining in size. Relatively few of the nation's 300,000-plus Protestant congregations are increasing the number of people who attend their worship services by at least 10 percent each year.

But the good news is that there are hundreds of churches across the nation that *are* growing. In studying the health of the Church, I have found many examples of churches that were determined to be relevant to the audience they sought to reach, and to incorporate growing numbers of people into their congregations. In their preparation for and pursuit of growth, they have learned much about what does and does not work in church growth today. These are the user friendly churches of the day.

What is a user friendly church? It is a church that is in touch with the needs of those it wants to serve. Just as a well-designed computer system enables even computer novices to use it effectively, user friendly churches enable a broad spectrum of people to come to know and serve the living God. None of the successful churches described in this book is interested in being user friendly in the sense of compromising the gospel or the historic faith of the church just to make friends with the age. Each of these churches affirms the gospel of Christ boldly and without apology. But they are equally firm in their intent to *listen* to the audiences they target, and to meet contemporary felt needs as the gospel directs.

This book builds on the fruits of these churches' hard-won insights. Why should you engage in the most costly form of research—trial and error—toward reinventing the wheel of church growth? Why should you retrace the steps that these growing churches have already taken? That is neither fulfilling, glorifying to God nor good stewardship. Instead, why not profit from an exposition of some of the most important principles that the user friendly congregations have developed, tested and proved to be valuable?

Much of the existing literature about church growth is of a case study nature, a simple description of a given church and what it did to engender numerical growth. Indeed, the purpose of many church growth books is to explicate existing church systems so that those same systems can be copied in other locations. The underlying assumption is that church growth can be duplicated by transplanting a successful plan from one church to another.

Imitation, as the saying goes, may be the sincerest form of flattery. But in the context of church growth, imitation is also the quickest route to doom. *Ministry by mimicry almost invariably results in deterioration, rather than growth.*

Why, then, write a book describing the success stories of two dozen churches drawn from across the nation?

Principles of Success
In this book I will take a different approach to describing cases in which churches have been successful. Rather than identify a church and describe its structure, its values and its performance, I will describe the *principles* that underlie the success of these

In the context of church growth, imitation is the quickest route to doom. Ministry by mimicry almost invariably results in deterioration, rather than growth.

churches. Having worked with a myriad of churches from coast to coast, I am certain that we do *not* need examples to *imitate.* What we *do* need are models to study so we can understand how transferable principles can be *adapted* to the environments in which we have been called to minister.

And I believe that we need to draw from the experience of churches that have grown both in numbers and in spiritual depth. One type of growth, either numerical or spiritual, without the other results in an imbalanced, unhealthy church.

Let me provide an example of one wonderful, healthy body that is mimicked all too often, to show that the problem is not the model but the way in which we frequently attempt to integrate the model into other ministries.

One of the congregations that is changing the nature of church ministry in America is Willow Creek Community Church. In just a single decade, WCCC grew to more than 14,000 weekly attenders, spawned countless imitators across the land and is partially responsible for a new way of thinking about what the local church can and should be. Having attended Willow Creek during my years in Illinois, I can say without any doubt that this is a real church: it has spiritual depth, biblical integrity and solid ministry priorities.

Thousands of pastors have come to the same conclusion. In fact, Willow Creek may well be the most copied church in America today. And that's the sad part.

Church leaders who have heard or read about the phenomenal success of Willow Creek make their exploratory pilgrimage to that church to observe and experience the totality of its ministry. They attend the services, talk to the staff, take notes about the facilities and programs, study the communication vehicles, examine the budget and so forth. More often than not, they return home and attempt to install Willow Creek II in their communities. Having witnessed an appealing model of success, they return to their own area and confidently begin to replicate what they studied.

Unfortunately, research of the results of numerous attempts to implant Willow Creek knock-offs around the country shows that most of these purists—leaders who have tried to implement the entire Willow Creek ministry in their area, lock, stock and barrel—have failed.

A church in New Mexico spent nearly a year preparing its Willow Creek impersonation. It launched its new program with great fanfare. Many people came. Few returned. Today that church is struggling to keep a single part-time pastor on retainer and to pay the rent to meet in a school gymnasium. Fewer than 50 people consistently attend.

A mid-sized congregation in Massachusetts was frustrated by its stagnation in numbers and attitude. After much deliberation, the church leaders concurred that some form of revitalization was necessary. The Willow Creek experience was chosen as the model for its renewal program. Steps were carefully taken to convert its ministry, based upon a traditional service format geared to churched people, into the type of seeker-oriented, contemporary ministry that has made Willow Creek so famous. It took less than a year after the transition was made for this northeastern church, despite good intentions and valiant efforts, to realize that they were worse off after the change than before.

In some cases where the Willow Creek model was attempted, the form of the new ministry attracted people—but not the intended people. A church in southern California, led by a dynamic young pastor who felt his ministry potential was limited by the traditional approach, developed a comprehensive plan for ministry based on the Willow Creek philosophy and strategy. His staff supported the move, church members eventually bought into the concept and the church shifted from a traditional service for the churched to a more modern service aimed at reaching the unchurched.

The congregation grew by 25 percent in less than two years. However, the pastor and staff concluded that the experiment had been a failure. Why? Because the newcomers were Christians from other churches. The saints had only been recirculated—the very outcome the church had hoped to avoid. Instead of finding the lost sheep, they had essentially stolen sheep from the pastures of other shepherds. The congregation attracted very few seekers, experienced just a handful of new conversions and had a total lack of understanding of the vision behind the switch from the existing mode of ministry to the new model.

Your Church Is Unique
In short, every church is faced with an absolutely unique set of circumstances to which it is called to minister. You cannot simply locate a growing church, identify the characteristics of that ministry and implement a carbon copy with the expectation of success. In America today, every church that wishes to impact lives has to be sensitive enough to those lives to mold a new, customized ministry dedicated to meeting the unduplicated needs of that target audience.

People are different, and they respond in different ways to the same stimuli. Seekers in northern Illinois are different from seekers in southern California. Evangelicals in Washington are different from evangelicals in Georgia. I can tell you from experience that unchurched baby boomers in Glendale, California, are a different breed from their counterparts just ten miles away in Tujunga.

With these practical realities in mind, then, this book is meant to outline a series of church growth principles that are working today and can be adapted to your situation. You can learn much from the experience of model churches. But you cannot grow by attempting to replicate the model down to the last element.

I have chosen not to reveal the names of the churches from which these principles were derived. The purpose is to prevent us from falling into our historic patterns: find out about a grow-

The tactics required to develop strong spiritual character...are very different from the tactics required to generate numerical growth.

ing church, make the exploratory pilgrimage and redesign our ministries to wholly incorporate one or more attractive aspects of that church. (In some cases, the pastors expressed the desire to remain anonymous, since they are already inundated with time-consuming requests from many church leaders for information and materials about their ministry.)

There are some facts about these churches, though, that you should know. The core of churches studied represent a broad spectrum of ministries. They are located in all four geographic regions of the nation; represent both charismatic and non-charismatic churches; reflect evangelical, fundamentalist and mainline bodies as well as both denominational and non-denominational churches; include congregations whose style of worship service ranged from contemporary rock-and-drama formats to "high church," traditional approaches; and involve congregations ranging in weekly attendance from 250 people to over 8,000. It was critical to encompass such a wide array of churches so that you are exposed to principles that transcend the finite limitations of denomination, location size and theological bent.

Start Fresh or Recast?

When I speak to groups of pastors about this information, they often ask about the difference between planting a new church and renewing an existing church using these perspectives and techniques. The fact is that it *is* substantially easier to start fresh than to recast an existing body into a new entity.

There are, however, examples of churches in which a stagnant body has had new life breathed into it through a change of direction or nature. It certainly takes a strong, visionary leader to make that change happen. Too often, a turnaround is attempted on the basis of methodology instead of a holistic view of ministry. Even in a newly planted church, realize that you cannot hope to have a *growing* church that also has *substance* if you rely only upon the methodology to create spiritual depth and staying power. The tactics required to develop strong spiritual character, we learned from these churches, are very different from the tactics required to generate numerical growth. Failure to pursue and achieve balance between those competing but complementary interests leads to an unhealthy church.

Choosing the Churches

Let me explain, too, how I chose the churches to be examined for this study. Each church was one which has come to the attention of my company, the Barna Research Group, through the research we conduct for and about churches in America. In a few cases, these were churches for whom we had done consulting. In other cases, they were churches used as models by the churches with whom we had contact. Some were churches we learned about through conversations with other church growth specialists or church leaders.

Each church had to meet two criteria to be included in the study. First, the congregation had to be growing numerically by at least 10 percent per year. We used average worship service attendance figures rather than membership figures for two reasons. First, churches tend to have different ways of preparing and counting members. Some churches count anyone who attends a service and fills out an attendance registration form. Others have candidates for membership take elaborate indoctrination classes and tests before being accepted. Some churches believe "once a member, always a member." Others have individuals sign on as members for a one year period, and require that they make a conscious decision to renew their membership each year.

More important, though, is our contention that membership is a meaningless comparative statistic. It is a concept born in another era. In America today, with the values of people changing rapidly and significantly, long-term loyalty and commitment are passe concepts. There are growing numbers of people who, even if they attend a church regularly and are active participants in the ministry of the Body, refuse to join the church.[1] Given this shift in behavior, we felt it made more sense to judge by the number of people *present* than by the number who have signed a piece of paper or persevered through a series of classes and meetings.

The second major criterion was that the church give ample evidence that its people are growing spiritually. America is a nation infatuated by form. Substance is less important than style or image to most of us. We ooh and ah at large numbers, and ignore the basis of those numbers. We are impressed by the seven-figure salaries of sports heroes, but remain oblivious to the thousands of hours those individuals have spent honing their skills to reach the top. Frequently, we learn of a church with thousands in attendance and assume that it is a thriving, substantial church.

What Is Success?

Unfortunately, we often gloss over a critical question: What is our definition of "success"? If we are speaking of the church, our source of that definition must be the Bible. From what I can find, the Bible never indicates that there is anything sacred about large numbers of people getting together as the Body of Christ. What it *does* suggest is that a church is a blessing if it is changing people's lives by bringing them into a deeper relationship with God, through faith in Christ and the indwelling power of the Holy Spirit. The church that blesses people in this way is a user friendly church.

I found some churches that, numerically, were growing rapidly. By some people's standards, these are the successful churches in America: big numbers, big budgets, widespread recognition. But upon closer examination, it was obvious why those churches were growing. Their spiritual depth was a mile long and an inch deep. Little commitment was expected from the people—and little was received. People were rarely challenged to make Christ the priority in their life—and consequently they rarely did so. Being a regular participant in those churches was a simple and joyous process, largely because so little was expected of them.

Those churches were excluded from the study. It's not hard to grow a huge congregation if all you want to do is give people a pleasing performance—the form of religion without the real substance. But I don't believe that is what the Bible is urging us to create as we attempt to be the salt of the earth.

Thus, the churches represented in this book showed evidence of spiritual depth. People were consistently exhorted to grow. Spiritual growth was the ultimate goal. *Numerical increase resulted from the manner in which that spiritual growth was facilitated.*

Ingredients for Development and Renewal

This book is not a total plan for ministry. It is a description of *the characteristics that these healthy, growing churches had in common.* Undoubtedly, each church had other factors that were important in its personality, structure, goals and performance. What I think is most useful, though, is to perceive those aspects that were invariably present in the congregations that seemed to be most vibrant.

The Church in America is in desperate need of a new model for the local church. We currently develop churches based on a model of ministry that was developed several hundred years ago, rejecting the fact that the society for which that model was designed no longer exists. The constant cry of the unchurched— "the church is irrelevant to the way I live"—cannot be addressed until the model itself is renewed to acknowledge that the times have changed. Our approach to meeting people's needs with the unchanging truths of the gospel must reflect our sensitivity to that change.[2]

This book, however, is *not* the description of that new model for the church. I believe that the principles uncovered through this study are important ingredients to be included in that model. But further testing needs to be done before the new model (or models) can be defined. In the meantime, the principles described in this book should help toward church renewal and development.

Finally, a warning. The churches studied were successful largely because they had a holistic perspective of ministry. Ministry was not an unrelated series of ideas, concepts, strategies and tactics. It was the outgrowth of a well-conceived, full-blown conception of what ministry to a person and to a community means. You may do yourself more harm than good if you simply pick and choose elements in these pages that you like, or those that would be easy to implement. Please invest sufficient time and reflection to explore how such changes might fit your style and philosophy of ministry. Ask about potential difficulties, and how you might articulate the shift such changes would mean for your church's vision of the ministry God has for it.

Notes
1. George Barna, *The Frog in the Kettle: What Christians Need to Know About Life in the Year 2000* (Ventura, CA: Regal Books, 1990), p. 133.
2. George Barna, *Never on a Sunday: The Challenge of Reaching the Unchurched* (Glendale, CA: Barna Research Group, 1990).

SECTION I PERSPECTIVE

Now Laban had two daughters; the name of the elder was Leah, and the name of the younger was Rachel. Leah's eyes were lovely, and Rachel was graceful and beautiful. Jacob loved Rachel . . . So Jacob served seven years for Rachel, and they seemed to him but a few days because of the love he had for her (Gen. 29:16-18,20, NRSV).

LIKE MANY OF OUR NATION'S MOST PROFITABLE CORPORATIONS, THE user friendly churches I studied had learned that *attitude* is an important key to progress and success. How they thought was just as important as what they did. Their actions were a consequence of their unique perspective on the meaning and being of a church. The way they perceived the world around them; how they thought of themselves in relationship to Christ, the world and each other; and the standards which they developed for evaluating who they were and what they did—all point to a very different outlook on life and ministry.

After reading about the components of the perspective that enabled these churches to grow, you may feel disappointed and unfulfilled. These churches broke no new ground. They simply did what many people would expect or encourage churches to do. Yet, the six characteristics we'll explore in the following chapters are noteworthy because these churches worked hard to master the key aspects of ministry perspective, with very favorable, if predictable, results. Attitude was not something they left to chance; it was a conscious goal toward which they strove with concerted energy.

These churches returned to the basics of ministry and discovered a refreshing liveliness and excitement in that simplicity. Yet, while the basic elements of their ministry were simple, they diligently pursued excellence in the performance of those basics. One of the battle cries of these churches was "Do it right, or don't do it at all." They were not content to simply get a difficult job done; they strove to do it superbly. They were not satisfied with doing what had always been done before, if there was a more effective means of reaching or impacting people. They never sat back and rested on their laurels as though they had achieved all that could be achieved. These churches maintained that they could always be doing their work more effectively, more efficiently, more extensively. They were convinced that Christ had singled them out to do an important and unique work.

Like Jacob working for Leah, these churches did not consider ministry a duty; it was a coveted, privileged, joyous opportunity. Every one of these congregations went through periods of discouragement and exhaustion. Yet, they invariably short-circuited those gray periods by refocusing their attention and energies on identifying new opportunities. Studying these churches was a tremendous personal blessing because it proved to me that ministry could be fun, exciting and rewarding—if you have the proper perspective. ➡

1 THE POWER OF A POSITIVE ATTITUDE

THE JAMISON FAMILY, NEW IN THE COMMUNITY, WAS SEARCHING FOR a church home. They were a little nervous, especially the kids, Josh and Katie. But the usher who shook their hands in greeting gave Josh a friendly wink as he turned to lead them to their seat, and the whole family relaxed. The organ was already playing, and people were finishing their whispered conversations as they settled down for the service. The minister's greeting was warm but not gushy. He caught the congregation's attention when he said he was giving everyone permission to "be noisy"— as long as they were making "a joyful noise to the Lord," quoting the psalm. The choir sang, an elder prayed. There was no contrived attempt to program a particular tone . . . but ten minutes into the service, without being able to say just why, the Jamisons knew they had found a home.

Like the Jamisons, when visitors attended any of the churches that were the focus of my studies, they could tell something was different. Apart from any differences in worship format, educational programs or style of buildings, visitors could sense that something made these churches unique. Often, they could not put their finger on that element, but they knew it was there—and, more importantly, they liked it.

The difference *was* hard to identify, largely because it was not tangible. But it clearly was a combination of factors related to a difference in *attitude*.

A VISION FOR MINISTRY

How do you evaluate an attitude? It is more than just the sum of the smiles, words and behaviors of those in the church body. I tried to understand what led to the apparent attitude within these congregations. Over time, it became clear that the attitude demonstrated by these people was *a response to the vision for ministry* that had drawn that body of people together. These churches were comprised of people, both clergy and laity, who had been exposed to God's vision for that body. That vision had been articulated by leaders who were genuinely enthusiastic about the potential of working through the church to change people's lives through the practical expression of the gospel.

The existence of this pro-ministry, we-can-do-it attitude within these churches was no accident. In all of the cases examined, the church leaders worked conscientiously to engender a positive attitude among the people. They did so in the ways they spoke; the news they imparted; the ways they carried themselves; the appearance and condition of the facilities; the tone of church communications; their ideas and actions related to church programs and policies; and the reports they gave concerning the performance of church programs. In fact, most of these churches specifically taught about the importance of attitude.

The teaching, by the way, was not a carefully designed, clever approach to manipulating people. It was an expression of the perspectives of the leaders within the church. Their ability to instill uplifting attitudes in the congregation grew out of their own belief in God's blessing. Their desire to serve Him wholeheartedly was contagious. How liberating it is, people learned, to have such dreams and such faith that obstacles simply become creative challenges! How refreshing it is to shed one's anxieties and replace them with visions of impact! Just as gloom can spread like wildfire, so can a positive attitude about the privilege and excitement of serving the living, active God.

Beyond such teaching, though, the attitude evident in these churches was an emotional response to a conscious, rational decision to accept ministry as the core of one's purpose in life. The people in many of the stagnant or declining churches I examined accepted the same intellectual principle about the primacy of ministry. That is, in their *minds* they *knew* they were supposed to make ministry their highest priority. But in their *hearts*, they didn't really *feel* it. When they engaged in activities designed to minister to others, they were frequently going through the motions. In the growing churches, there was an integration of mind and heart related to ministry. They did not engage in outreach because it was the right thing to do. They engaged in outreach because they *wanted* to do it, and they believed that it would honor God.

This way of looking at the world and understanding their purpose for living radically transformed how these people thought, talked and behaved. The vision for ministry served as a filter for perception and response. The vision was described to them winsomely, and their attitude was a manifestation of their acceptance of the vision as their reason for being.

ANATOMY OF AN ATTITUDE

What are the components of this special attitude? First, these people were *excited about ministry*. They thought church was the only place worth being on Sunday morning. They couldn't wait for the service, and they got pumped up for the rest of the week by taking part in the worship experience. Other experiences related to the church—Sunday School, midweek services, small group studies, community outreach ministries—heightened their excitement about what God had called them to do.

What was so exciting about these activities, which are common to most churches? People were excited to learn new things about God, about their relationship with Christ, about the work of the Holy Spirit. They were excited to discover ways in which they could be used by God to change the lives of other people. They were excited to hear about the impact that the Church, worldwide, was having through a variety of approaches to ministry.

To their credit, the leaders of these user friendly churches placed the information and techniques they imparted within a lively context. They understood that part of their role as a church leader or as a teacher was to motivate, in addition to imparting factual information. The sense of exuberance that grew among the laity reflected the fact that the leaders were themselves excited about the work of the church, the opportunities before their own congregation and the knowledge that God wanted to use that church and its people to be a blessing to the world.

A Ministry to Others

Overall, the people at these churches were thrilled to be part of a body of believers that not only cared about ministry, but was out in the world doing the Lord's work, and seeing the fruits of their labors. To them, ministry did not simply mean being ministered *to*; it was just as critical that they use their gifts and resources to minister to others.

There is also much to be said for people feeling that they are part of a winning team. Adults these days are too busy and under too much pressure to cheerfully and willingly offer their free time to activities that continually fail. The prospect of being associated with an activity—especially a spiritual activity—that is having a positive influence on people, or otherwise resulting in victory, will in itself motivate enthusiasm, excitement and interest. Like it or not, success breeds success. But part of the challenge to these churches was to enable their people to perceive the success of their efforts.

Adults these days are too busy and under too much pressure to cheerfully and willingly offer their free time to activities that continually fail.

In addition, these were people who were *passionate about out-reach*. They were more than simply happy to be doing the Lord's work; they were inspired. Their perspective was that nothing could be more important than enabling others to understand Scripture, to make a commitment to Jesus Christ and to grow in their faith. They saw every event in their lives as having a hand in better enabling them to reach others for Christ. They looked upon life as an opportunity to serve God.

Further, these people believed in a God who knows no bounds, and they entered ministry full of expectancy. They believed that they, personally, made a difference by serving Christ wholeheartedly. They had no doubt that God would use their simple efforts to reap great returns. And they recognized that being a part of a body of believers that is on fire to transform the world is a blessing that could not be matched.

A Spirit of Expectancy

Let's be realistic about all of this. Certainly, not everyone in these churches gave evidence of such an attitude. As in every church, a few cynics and grumblers were sprinkled throughout the lot. But, led by a pastor who modeled positive attitudes, the body was literally transformed into a force of conviction and joy. Their exuberance and anticipation made a difference. The body was dominated by a positive, expectant spirit.

This buoyant corporate attitude was enough to motivate some of the less spiritually-inclined to reexamine their lives and their relationship with Christ, to become more excited, passionate and expectant. In reality, it also caused some people to leave the church. My observation (although I have no hard data to support the contention) is that those who fled were generally individuals who had been in the mainstream of the congregation for many years. The church may have had substantial life at some point, but much of that energy had long since been depleted, and these individuals became accustomed to a congregation that was relatively lifeless. As a result, they felt uncomfortable in the presence of active Christianity.

The very spirit of excitement and expectancy that leads to a growing church is often preceded by a personal confrontation with the fear of the unknown. What if God can't do those things which we're counting on Him to do? What if I have to change the way I live to be a real man of God? What if I have to reorder my priorities in life? The threat of having to address such issues undoubtedly drove some long-term church people out the back door. It probably scared the daylights out of some nonbelieving visitors, too.

Growing churches typically expect every individual to make a decision about the importance of personal spiritual growth. In such an environment, although the tenor may be upbeat and positive, those people who are more interested in attending church than in growing in their relationship with Christ will frequently leave in favor of a less demanding environment.

On balance, though, the evidence suggests that most people are attracted to a church that overtly demonstrates such vitality and zeal. Rather than merely providing a forum for teachers to describe the potential of a healthy church, these are people who fulfill that potential by translating God's vision for the church in the midst of a hurting and dying world into a real and significant presence in that world.

Please understand that these were not simply giddy, mindless, "positive thinking" groups. At congregations driven by the "positive thinking" approach, there is often the assumption that people can overwhelm their environment and create the desired outcomes by sheer force of attitude. In the growing churches the perspective was that the evidence of God's blessings in their midst, in response to their prayers and hard work, was reason to have an expectant and positive attitude. Their attitude was not the substance of their ministry. Their attitude was a response to the blessing of being involved in life-changing ministry activities, and their anticipation of success was based on what God was able to do through them.

ATTITUDES THAT WERE ABSENT

Perhaps just as important as the attitudes that were discernible are some attitudes that were conspicuous by their absence. People at the growing churches were less likely to be skeptical about the potential for impacting the community. They saw success firsthand and had no reason to believe that God would not continue to bless the efforts of the church. Even those who harbored doubts thought twice about voicing their fear-based concerns.

Naturally, there were some people in the body with negative perceptions. However, unjustifiably negative attitudes were generally unable to gain a foothold in these churches. This does not mean that the leaders were closed to examining the risk or down-side of any program or activity. These were astute decision-makers, who moved forward with suitable levels of caution and sensitivity. However, they would not allow the unbridled fear of failure to be a wet blanket on the fires of ministry passion that burned within the congregation.

Another missing attitude was that of complacency about God's response to His people. In many stagnant churches there is a brief period of fervent prayer, work and desire for a specific outcome. The answer from God may come much later in time, after the passion has died, or it may not come in the desired form. Yet, when the answer arrives, these people shrug it off as though it is no longer significant. "Yeah, now that you mention it, I guess God did that, didn't He?" or "Oh, that's nice" are expressions that might characterize the typical response to His provision.

In the growing churches, however, God's response to expressions of need or concern were consistently acknowledged. His reaction was grounds for people to maintain their excitement about His willingness to use them for His purposes.

TAKING INVENTORY

Every organization or group of people has a corporate personality. Unless leaders consciously shape this character, it will likely emerge as a reflection of the strongest individuals in the group. Has your church determined that part of its mission is to create the desired personality? This entails the intentional development of a proper attitude. Who within the church is responsible for making this happen, and what strategies will be deployed to guide the shaping of that personality?

Most people are followers. If the people in your church do not seem truly excited or passionate about ministry, is it because they do not have a leader who models those traits for them? In other words, is there someone in the church who is a role model? Is that individual setting the pace for a proper attitude?

Just as important is providing the church with reasons to feel excited and forward-looking. Some churches engage in prayer and programs that are designed to gain God's blessing— but when the blessing is provided, they fail to acknowledge it, and to communicate that response to the congregation. How well are you informing people of the many ways in which God is taking care of your needs?

It's hard to get enthusiastic about a ministry that has no results over which to get excited. But it is impossible to become passionate, much less excited, about a ministry that does not have a vision for ministry that undergirds its efforts. If your church lacks passion, is it because the people do not understand the vision? Is it because the church itself does not have a clear sense of God's vision for outreach?

What about the people in every congregation who simply refuse to become enthusiastic? In successful churches, these people are loved and accepted, but they are also firmly challenged to think and speak in new ways. They are encouraged to be positive, and to see the glass as half full rather than half empty. Because it is natural for some people to disbelieve until proof is provided, leaders of successful churches develop strategies for handling such attitudes in advance. They have defined doubt and negativity as enemies of effective ministry. They take the offensive when such attitudes assert their presence. And they reinforce those people whose attitudes are consistent with the pulse of the church.

Does your church have such strategies in place?

2 BUILDING LIVING STONES

A WOMAN WE'LL CALL MRS. CRAWFORD APPROACHED THE MINISTER hesitantly after the Sunday morning sermon. A widow, she had begun to visit shut-ins a couple of years ago. Recently she had discovered several single elderly people in her neighborhood who were not receiving adequate nourishment. Ordinarily they were in fairly good health. But recent foul weather had made it hard for them to do their regular grocery shopping, and Mrs. Crawford wondered if the church could help.

"Dr. McVey," she said, "thank you for the sermon. Could I speak to you a moment about some needs I've discovered? Several elderly people in my neighborhood could use some help with their meals, and I thought maybe the church could help."

"Fine, fine!" the minister replied heartily. "You need to see Gary Traylor about that. He's in touch with the ecumenical Meals-on-Wheels program here in town. He might get them enrolled in that. Thanks for caring!" And with that Dr. McVey was off to speak to the choir leader.

Mrs. Crawford was disappointed. The people she was in touch with needed only temporary help. Plus, they needed people contact as much as meals, and she had hoped it could come from individuals in her own church. And if the truth were known, Mrs. Crawford herself needed the personal contact, too. She heaved a deep sigh and went home to a dark house.

PROGRAMS VS. PEOPLE

America is a unique nation in many ways. One example is its emphasis on the development of *systems* to manage problems. This has been one of the key factors underlying the economic strength of the nation. Education, manufacturing, distribution, government—virtually every aspect of our lives is shaped by the systems and organization structures developed to address the need for productivity and efficiency.

Anyone who evaluates churches notices that they, too, have embraced the systems approach to organizational behavior. When a challenge arises, churches attempt to design a system that will handle the situation effectively. We refer to these systems as our programs. Dr. McVey's mind immediately linked the needs Mrs. Crawford tried to share with a program—the very good program of Meals on Wheels.

The systems approach has helped American culture thrive by sustaining order in what would otherwise be a chaotic and disorganized mass. Aware of this positive influence, many churches have unknowingly applied a systems approach to their ministry, and the result is a highly structured, program-rich ministry.

The Ministry of People

There is only one problem with this strategy. *Ministry is not about programs. Ministry is about people.* While Dr. McVey's program-oriented approach has its place, he missed the more acute people needs Mrs. Crawford represented.

Jesus did not minister through programs. The early church did not appoint program managers. The Bible never exhorts us to create programs. Jesus, the apostles, the Bible—all indicate by word or deed that our focus is to be on people, through meaningful relationships.

This principle was recognized in the successful churches studied. Their emphasis was on people, not programs. When opportunities for ministry emerged, the most common response was for leaders to encourage individuals to get involved in the life of the person who required support.

Often, churches identify a need and institute a program. Once implemented, programs tend to perpetuate themselves. Leaders often fail to assess how well the program is addressing the need that prompted the response originally, and how the target audience responds to the program. Some churches fool themselves into believing that because they have a program in place, they are doing ministry. What they are really doing is *programming.*

Ministry happens when a person's needs are met. Sometimes a program will facilitate that ministry. Sometimes it does not.

User friendly churches consistently demonstrated the ability to identify individuals within the church who were able to minister to people with a special need. The church actively encouraged those people to use their gifts and talents to do the ministry to which they were called, regardless of whether a program existed to foster such an outreach.

These churches did not look at people's expressed needs first and foremost as opportunities for creating programs. They perceived those needs as opportunities for one person to minister to another. If anything, programs were developed around a ministry that already existed. *It was rare in growing churches for programs to precede existing forms of outreach.*

POSITIVE PROGRAMMING

When Are Programs Needed?

Programs did, of course, emerge in the healthy churches. There were three dominant justifications for launching new programs.

First, by offering a program, more people were likely to know about the existence of the type of support available through that ministry, and therefore greater numbers of people could be served. In some ways, having a program made the process of seeking help easier: there was a designated time or place at which people skilled in helping would be readily available.

A second justification was that establishing a program was a way of acknowledging the breadth of need for such outreach. This enabled the church to involve more people in that form of ministry, and allowed them to provide some consistency in methods of helping people in need.

The third reason for a new program was that some needs required special expertise in order to provide effective, healthy outreach. This was especially true in some areas related to counseling. Dealing with the deep emotional needs of people is an art that requires leaders with great skill and compassion. To entrust such outreach to amateurs could potentially create more injury than healing. Thus, while programs were not always the desirable solution to needs, in some aspects of ministry the need to protect people and serve them properly called for a programmatic approach.

Expendable Programs

The growing churches, true to their flexible structure, also believed that *all programs were expendable.* Regardless of who started a program, how long it had been in existence, how many other churches had such a ministry, the number of staff people whose ministries were directly entwined with the outreach or whose pet project the program was, programs that were ineffective ministries became ex-programs.

There are many church programs in place today that were initiated on the basis of good intentions, or that at one time served specific needs quite satisfactorily. Today, however, many of those same programs actually *inhibit* ministry. The existence of the program allows people to sign up or become part of the

A program that was not pulling its own weight was axed from the program log without anguish and anxiety.

ministry team associated with the program, and hide behind that affiliation. Merely being associated, even in a nominal way, with an existing program enables many people to feel that they have fulfilled their ministry obligation. Unless a church has established very specific criteria for involvement in ministry, it is possible for the individual to feel exonerated from duty by the simple act of signing up. Associating with a program allows them to add a missing credential to their profile. Since they then can hide within the framework of an existing program, they are more likely to escape real accountability.

At the successful churches, this overstructured approach to ministry—the "program sanctuary" syndrome which gave people shelter from the need to really minister to others—had little hope of making inroads. A program that was not pulling its own weight was axed from the program log without anguish and anxiety.

To their credit, successful churches also measured their programs by a different statistical yardstick than most churches. At growing churches, a program was deemed successful according to how many changed lives resulted from the outreach.

This differs from the experience of stagnant churches, where a program is usually evaluated according to how many people are involved as either leaders or participants. Unfortunately, while many people may be involved, the program may become simply a social clique or a safety net, rather than an effective outreach.

Outreach vs. Inreach

User friendly churches also championed an entirely different philosophy about ministry than do many churches. Over the course of time, it is easy for a church to become ingrown, focusing on its own people and their concerns. Successful churches took a different tack, involving people in real ministry. They tended to believe that the most desirable form of ministry was outreach, not inreach. Toward that end, they taught their people that the best way to solve their own needs and problems was by focusing on serving others. Less self-absorption, they found, leads to a healthier perspective about the significance and severity of one's own dilemmas.

Several of the pastors at growing churches indicated that they had faced serious struggles trying to get people to focus on others instead of on themselves. "You have to realize," one pastor explained, "that many of these people came here in the first place because they needed help. We had ministry-minded laity who were waiting for the chance to help them. The dilemma is that this person-intensive solution becomes seductive. Once someone focuses on you, on your needs, and makes you the center of attention, it's hard to give that up. In today's world, you don't get to be the center of attention very often. Convincing someone who has had that type of healing and support to turn it around and experience the fulfillment of ministering to others instead is not an easy sell."

Pastors and associate pastors at several of the churches confronted this dilemma by trying to consistently recognize, applaud and encourage laity who were involved in one-on-one ministry. These clergy did little to organize programs or allow programs to take on a life of their own. Instead, they attempted to create opportunities and an environment in which people were freed of structures and regulations, and supported in their attempts to be a living resource to those in need. As one pastor described it, "My role is to equip them to minister, then to support them as they are doing it. The paperwork just has to pile up. My primary responsibility is to spend time with people, either equipping them or encouraging them as they are using those gifts."

TAKING INVENTORY

Suppose you were asked to list every program undertaken by your church, and then to identify how many people's lives had been substantially influenced by each program in the past year. If you were then asked to close down all of the programs which had not truly affected any lives in the past year, how many programs would you lose? What would it do to your church to go on a program diet, losing those unnecessary programs that absorb precious resources?

How often are the programs in your church evaluated? Who is responsible for the evaluations? And what is the basis for the evaluation? Hopefully, your church seeks to determine what type of impact the program has on lives, not just how many people take part in the program. Keep an eye on the number and nature of programs that come into existence. It is so easy for a church to get a bloated program roster and give the illusion of ministry, when what is really happening is the development of niches in which people can feel comfortable, rather than challenged.

What is the balance of programs within your church between those focused on the needs of your congregation and those emphasizing the needs of people outside of the church? If all of your programs are designed to minister only to the people who belong to your congregation, chances are good that you are breeding ministry paralysis. Seek ways to promote forms of outreach, whether through programs or individual efforts, that target not only the felt needs of the people within the walls of your church, but also those who are on the outside looking in.

The leaders of successful churches unanimously concurred that one of their most important roles was that of being a ministry cheerleader. If you are a church leader, how many meetings have you had in the past week in which you reviewed members' personal ministry and sought to encourage them to continue their outreach? Your calling is to impact people's lives. That requires more than preaching sermons, teaching classes and administrating the affairs of the church. These functions are vitally important; but not more important than how you build up your congregation for ministry.

3 | YOU CAN ONLY DO SO MUCH

In some ways, the story of the Brazleton Copier Co. (not its real name) is the story of American business in the last decade. Will it also become the sad story of many churches?

A privately owned company, Brazleton was so good at manufacturing and distributing its product that, near its plant in Pittsburgh where business leaders all knew the Brazleton family, it outsold Xerox copiers by two to one.

Giddy with its success, a new management team decided to go public. With the money from shares sold on the stock exchange, these visionaries bought out two small computer printer companies—one in New York and the other in California. After all: aren't copiers and printers sister products?

By means of hostile takeovers, leveraged buyouts and corporate mergers, Brazleton expanded into FAX machines, then telephone equipment, then video cameras, television and radio manufacturing and finally satellites for business use. After all: aren't all these products communications equipment, and in the same family?

No, the Brazleton Copier Co. found that the products were more like cousins than sisters. Each required differing technology, different marketing techniques, different customer expectations regarding distribution and service. One by one the new additions to the Brazleton family of products failed. Furthermore, the original copier side of the business began to falter because management's attention was on the new and glitzy expansion products. Now the company has pulled back to its home office. Ninety-five percent of the workers it hired during its expansion phase are no longer with the company, victims of the several layoffs required for survival. Nursing its wounds and heavily in debt, Brazleton is now trying to recapture the local market for copiers that it lost to Xerox.

When business analysts look back at the '80s to evaluate the long-term outcome of merger mania and the buyout binge, they will surely conclude that bigger was not better. Expansion through diversification seemed to be a wise move; but more often than not the result was a polyglot of companies that had little in common, no functional purpose for being joined together and generating more chaos and diseconomies of scale than they provided tangible benefits for the stockholders.

The lesson learned was that an organization is most successful not when it seeks to become the biggest or the broadest, but when it strives to be the best in its own focused area of expertise.

FOCUSING THE VISION

All Things to All People?

Sadly, most churches have yet to understand the application of this principle to their ministry. Simply put, *a church cannot be all things to all people.* When Paul wrote that he became "all things to all men" (1 Cor. 9:22, *NIV*), he was stressing the importance of contextualizing his message and ministry. He was not, as some church leaders suggest, pushing every single congregation to try to satisfy each need of every individual who comes into contact with that church.

In speaking with pastors of declining churches, a common

thread was their desire to do something for everybody. They had fallen into the strategic black hole of creating a ministry that looked great on paper, but had no ability to perform up to standards. Despite their worthy intentions, they tried to be so helpful to everyone that they wound up being helpful to no one. Their laudable objectives and resulting frustrations were evident in the words of one of the pastor who said, "I just don't understand it. My only desire is to serve Him. I do my best to be there for everyone. Nothing seems to have a lasting impact, though. Our numbers are declining, our impact in the community is virtually nil. It just doesn't make sense."

In a world filled with hurting people, we want to be the solution. Having been touched by the love of Christ in our own lives, it is only natural that we want to return the favor by sharing that love with others by being the answer to their every need. As a church, we are anxious to be on the spot, sharing the love of Christ and the truth of the gospel with everyone. The temptation is to try to satisfy every need that people can identify.

A Specific Mission
Even the growing, healthy churches I studied frequently struggled with this concept. Believe me, it is even more tempting to try to provide one-stop spiritual shopping when your church has had an unbroken string of successes.

However, the stark reality is that every church has limited resources, and has been called to accomplish a specific mission. Despite the urge to be all things to all people, the successful churches resisted that impulse to be the answer to everyone's every problem by focusing on their vision for ministry, by reaffirming their commitment to quality, and by recognizing their limitations. If they were to devote themselves to meeting every need in their marketplace, they would dissipate their resources and have no impact—the very tragedy that has befallen the majority of the Protestant churches in America. In general, these growing congregations refused to be enticed into areas of ministry in which they discerned no special calling. Instead, they concentrated on doing what they knew, beyond a doubt, they were called to do.

One congregation I studied grew from a handful of people to several hundred within less than three years. They did so without a ministry to children and teens. This was not because they saw no need for such a ministry. The pastor was certain that if they had such a ministry in operation, the church would probably add several hundred new members in a short period. They planned to launch such a ministry, but only when they knew what they were doing, and were assured that they would do it with excellence. "The last thing I want to do is drive those parents and their kids out of here because we weren't really ready to deal with them," the pastor said. "Once we have our act together, we'll launch our youth ministry. Until then, I'd be doing this church and those families a disservice by allowing us to offer a half-baked, premature outreach."

True to his expectations, when the church did launch the youth and children's program six months later, it was instrumental in ushering in more than 200 new regular attenders within six months.

MEASURED EXPANSION

Does this disciplined recognition of the church's limitations mean that user friendly churches never grew beyond the ministry boundaries that were set at the time they started to grow? Absolutely not! However, the history of these churches has been to expand the nature of their ministry slowly. Generally, they are able to attract a sufficient number of people to the church by doing a few key ministries with excellence, rather than doing many things merely adequately. By expanding too quickly, they would have lost the strong base upon which they built an effective outreach.

The successful churches resisted the impulse to be the answer to everyone's *every* problem by focusing on their vision for ministry, reaffirming their commitment to quality and recognizing their limitations.

How do those new areas of ministry make their way from idea to reality within the existing fabric of the church? The cycle seems somewhat predictable. In each healthy church, there was first the recognition of a gap in ministry services provided. Next came a determination by those who were concerned about the gap to pray about the ability and means to plug the gap. Finally the church was able to accumulate sufficient resources, in response to specific prayer and a plan for action, to merit the initiation of that area of ministry. At that point, and only at that point, was the new ministry introduced.

HANDLING "REJECTION"

Even beyond the issue of not being spread too thin, the healthy churches exhibited yet another uncommon notion. If a person visited the church and didn't like it or didn't feel comfortable there, that was perfectly acceptable. A couple of the pastors called it a response that was "ordained by God" and "in the best interests of our congregation and of that individual." There was no lost sleep over the fact that they had been rejected by visitors.

"Look, we've worked long and hard at trying to provide anyone who spends time with us with a very positive, pleasant experience," said one pastor in defense of his lack of concern about not "capturing" every prospect. "I know that what we do is right for some people and not right for others. I can live with that as long as I know we're doing what God has created this congregation to do, and that we are doing it better than anyone else. Really, if the person doesn't feel this is the right place, I don't *want* him here. He needs to be in the place that God has created for him, so he can be a healthy, growing, giving part of the overall body."

In my own research, the facts seemed to bear out this perspective. Even those who decided that the church was not what they sought rarely had an unpleasant experience when they visited. Some were tempted to return, because of the environment and the attitude of the congregation, but nevertheless decided to look elsewhere for a ministry that was better suited to meeting their own needs and style.

"More power to them," said another pastor from one of the growing churches. "As long as those folks leave with a good taste in their mouth, feeling that if what we showed them was Christianity then it ain't bad after all, then I don't feel we failed. Chances are that the good time they had with us will encourage them to find a church that's right for them. If they stayed here they never would have been happy or fulfilled. And they'd probably be a pain in the neck to us, a distraction while we're trying to keep our focus on the people we are trying to reach."

The leaders of the user friendly churches were at peace with this amicable parting of ways with visitors. (Often, this was a major source of disagreement in the early stages of the church's ministry, but was settled through prayer, study and faith that God would bless the church in a unique way.) While they were naturally disappointed that their ministry did not satisfy a visitor's needs, they were confident that there was another church in God's plan that would meet those needs. They were also confident that if they tried to meet every need of every person who entered their doors, their successful outreach would turn into a watered down, paralyzed ministry of little value to anyone. It would be better to reach a few people with great impact, they felt, than to reach many people with no impact.

The pastors and staff of these churches had a good sense of the other ministries in their geographic area. They were quite willing to suggest other churches for people to try when the visitors' experience at the growing church had not met their needs or expectations. Once again, driven by God's vision, and inspired by a passion for their calling, these pastors had little sadness about recommending another church to someone. They perceived the Church to be the entire Body of believers, not just their own congregation. To them, the Church transcended congregational or denominational lines. Their role was to help

God's Church grow in whatever ways He allowed that to happen. Thus, they were willing to guide a person to a nearby church better suited to that person's needs. They would happily cooperate with other churches in the area which had significant ministries, and expected the same cooperative spirit from the pastors of other churches.

"Yes, I want my congregation to grow," explained one pastor from a rapidly growing church in the midwest. "But if I really believe that we are all part of the Church of Christ, I have to prove it in my ministry and my heart. I would rather know that someone was won to the Kingdom, than lost to the world. If I do things that facilitate anything less, even if it is simply trying to build up my own membership numbers, I'm a hypocrite."

This same philosophy was evident in the outreach programs of the church, not just in efforts to attract visitors. These churches recognized the numerous opportunities for addressing needs in the community and the world, but they restricted their outreach to those ministries to which they felt called by God, and for which they had sufficient resources to do an excellent job.

Was this limiting God, or failing to trust Him for their needs? Not in the perception of these pastors. They saw their decision as a means of maximizing their influence: doing their core ministries superbly, providing evidence of the effectiveness of the church, and establishing new opportunities to tell people that the impressive work of the church is a reflection of God's leading and blessing. They also believed that if every church were to assume this attitude and concentrate its resources in the areas to which it had been called, the many existing needs of the population would be addressed by the entire Church community, instead of by a relative handful of churches.

TAKING INVENTORY

If the people who live in your community were asked to identify the two or three unique qualities or characteristics of your church, what would those factors be? What would you say are the ministry strengths of your church? Is your church truly concentrating on doing those few things with excellence, or is it diluting its impact by trying to have something for everybody? The experience of the user friendly churches was that they were better off having depth of ministry than breadth of ministry, even if it meant the temporary absence of an outreach in an area of need.

It is inevitable that some people will visit your church and never come back. Reflect on the reaction of your leaders to such an experience. Think about the information they consider when evaluating such circumstances, and how they analyze that information. In many churches, any warm body is seen as fair game and a prime prospect for the church. Has your church come to grips with the reality that perhaps the individual was not meant to be a permanent part of your church? Would such a perception cause concern among your key leaders? Do your leaders react rashly to having the church rejected by visitors, calling for immediate changes in the church? Is there an attempt to understand why some visitors choose not to attach to the congregation—and an effort to assist them in finding the right church?

There are times when it makes sense for a church to consider initiating a new arm of outreach. Such decisions are handled differently by various churches. Yet, successful churches have policies for how they evaluate the merit of initiating new ministries. How does your church handle the possibility of beginning a new outreach? Is the prospect of being spread too thin, or of not having sufficient resources to do the ministry with excellence, primary considerations?

4 TAKING PRIDE IN THE PRODUCT

A MAJOR REASON FOR THE SUCCESS OF THE CHURCHES I STUDIED WAS their determination to remain sensitive to the people they were seeking to reach and serve. This meant understanding how people in their community live, and what needs they have which a church might address. It also meant staying informed about how people respond to the church itself: the level of quality with which the church's people, programs, direction, benefits, opportunities for service and facilities are impacting the community.

THE QUEST FOR QUALITY

An Openness to Feedback

One church seeking to grow invited a puppeteer from a nearby city to present a program for youth. The young man was a good ventriloquist, his message was doctrinally sound and he captured the attention of the youth. Furthermore, there was an overflow audience. But he made the mistake of singing! His zeal to present a "multi-media" program was greater than his singing talent. During feedback following the program people complained about off-key notes, an untrained voice and unfamiliar songs during audience sing-along time. No doubt God will reward the young man for doing his best; but He did not reward the host church with favorable feedback on the quality of the program.

Still, the church is to be commended for *asking* for a critique of the program. It did not assume that "a good crowd" automatically meant successful ministry to youth. Gaining reliable feedback was an ingrained part of the ministry process at the user friendly churches I surveyed. They were persistent in their search for answers to questions about the impact of the ministry, and about how well the ministry was doing on an objective measure of performance.

A Qualitative Perspective

What distinguished them from the typical church was not simply the quest for feedback from a wide range of sources. Even when they received information, they tended to interpret it differently than do the leaders at most churches. Raw numbers are necessary but insufficient measures of ministry quality, they claim, because statistics such as attendance figures represent a limited, one-dimensional perspective. They were just as interested in gaining a *qualitative* understanding as they were in having a *quantitative* perspective on how well the church was doing.

It wasn't that the pastors of these growing churches were disinterested in pastoring a church that was growing numerically. But numerical growth, in their view, was an outgrowth of a strong ministry. Their underlying belief was that *quantity is a result of quality.* While they were usually keenly aware of the numbers of people involved in their church, their primary consideration was whether or not the church was providing the quality of outreach that would keep these individuals returning and growing. Quality, in other words, was both a means and an end in effective church outreach.

This focus on quality relates to another key principle of their philosophies about church growth. Most of the pastors of these

The leaders of successful churches emphatically declared that it
is possible to have a church that
swells numerically, but has little
ministry value.

growing churches suggested that a key to numerical growth was not just the acquisition of new members, but also the retention of existing believers. They felt that it was tough enough, in the context of real ministry (not costless Christianity), to get out-siders to visit and evaluate their church. On top of that they felt the need to provide a ministry that was so well-defined and carried out with such excellence that people felt compelled not only to return for more, but to want to become actively involved in the ministry.

Quality was not just a word used to communicate the impres-sion that the church was in tune with people's needs and expec-tations. The concept of quality seemed to involve five major aspects for the healthy churches I studied.

Integrity. The message conveyed by the church must not be simply interesting and useful, but also an accurate reflection of God's Word to us. A church which confuses biblical truth with personal perceptions leaves the congregation open to incidents of misinterpretation, confusion and misguided response.

Excellence in effort. People are attracted to organizations whose product or service is provided at the highest levels of quality. Since the Church has been called to represent God to the world, we ought to reflect His excellence in all that we do, recognizing that we are ultimately serving Him, and that He deserves nothing less than our best possible effort.

Consistency. Sometimes, churches send mixed signals to those who are involved with its ministry. A church that wishes to bond with its people and be certain of supporting their per-sonal spiritual growth must have a clear notion of what it believes, how to effectively and consistently communicate that belief and how to live in harmony with the message it has sent.

Credibility. Unless the people who hold positions of respon-sibility within the church have a high level of credibility, the information and example they seek to pass along will have lit-tle interest to the congregation. Further, the pastors interviewed on this matter indicated that because the pace and tone of the ministry is often set or influenced by the pastoral staff, they must be beyond reproach or else jeopardize the entire ministry.

Reliability. When church members bring their friends to church, or if they are personally agonizing over a crisis in their lives, the church must be available and prepared to offer realistic and meaningful solutions. Once a person can no longer count on the church to be there when he needs it, its viability as a support mechanism for the individual is undermined.

THE IMPORTANCE OF BIBLICAL MINISTRY

Blending these traits into a philosophy of ministry was important to the leaders of the growing churches. To provide anything less than the highest possible quality, as defined by these characteristics, was thought to be cheating the people out of what is rightfully theirs.

The leaders of these successful churches emphatically declared that it is possible to have a church that swells numerically, but has little ministry value. Several pastors indicated that they believed this condition is becoming increasingly common these days. Regardless of the trend, each man cited one or two examples of such churches, as though the substance of those congregations had been indelibly etched upon their minds, serving as a model of what *not* to become.

The pastor of a large evangelical church in the South declared, "I'll bet that if you took every church in this country that is growing quickly, and evaluate what they really teach, more often than not you'd find that those churches only use the name of Christianity, but aren't really teaching accurately from the Bible." He went on to say, "I'm not disputing the likelihood that what they do in those churches they do very well. The problem is that what they're doing well is not real Christian ministry. They may call it that, to borrow some of the social credibility of the faith, but then they water down the teaching to make it so palatable that it has no real substance."

Unwilling to Compromise

Christian churches, like any institutions attempting to gain a following, run the risk of attracting people who simply want to be at the "right" place, numbered among those who attend the "hot" church. Often, large and growing churches gain numbers by compromising what they believe in order to maintain their growth. The successful churches studied, though, were adamant about not compromising their beliefs, even if it meant their growth came to a grinding halt.

One senior pastor, whose church serves as a model for many new churches around the nation, explained how he purposefully tries to reduce the numbers of his congregation out of fear that they haven't counted the cost of following Christ. He expressed his relief that his church's rapid growth immediately tapered off after a series of particularly challenging sermons. Although his typical sermons invariably wed people's needs with biblical truth, he regularly uses periods of "hard" messages to confront members with the cost of discipleship, even at the expense of a reduction in the numbers of people coming to the church.

"It's not that I don't want those people to be part of our congregation," he said. "It's just that when that many people volunteer to be a part of our group, I wonder if they heard, I mean *really* heard what I was saying. Authentic Christianity has a high cost attached to it. And I know that paying the price is not a popular thing to do in America today. When the numbers seem to swell a bit too fast, I figure it's time to preach a series that really gets down and emphasizes the tough stuff of the faith. If they hear that and come back for more, then I feel okay about it."

Even though their churches had gained recognition for fast growth, one of the greatest tensions which the pastors of these churches admitted to struggling with was the conflict between the desire to reach more people (i.e., numbers) and the fear of losing the commitment to excellence that enabled the church to attract people in the first place (i.e. quality).

STAYING OPEN TO FEEDBACK

Avoiding the Denial Syndrome

How do these pastors keep from falling into the trap of being merely average (or worse)? One of the most refreshing factors that distinguished successful churches was their refusal to get into the denial syndrome. Many times, weaknesses in various aspects of ministry are denied by church leaders, in the hope that the weakness will simply disappear without having to be acknowledged or confronted. Of course, the problem rarely disappears as hoped. The weakness typically becomes more glaring, until finally it undermines the ministry.

But in the user friendly churches, there was almost a passion for identifying weaknesses and developing practical and efficient solutions to those soft spots. Both pastors and congregations were always open to hearing new evidence about how the church was doing. These leaders did not always immediately or readily accept bad news, or news that might initially seem discouraging. However, it seems that they did have the ability to provide an objective judgment about the situation after reflecting upon the information for a short time.

Objective Feedback

Another difference that stood out was that these churches' leaders insisted that the feedback not come just from the professionals whose jobs were on the line and thus had a vested interest or prejudiced view (i.e., church staff). They wanted feedback from the people whose lives must be touched by what the church is doing. Each user friendly church had a time of review and response following Sunday's activities. During the review, each staff person reporting feedback had to provide input from "credible" sources. The personal reflections of the staff members held some weight, but input from the laity was deemed of equal or greater value.

In most of the growing churches, surveys were used as a regular part of the evaluation process. Some of the churches used congregation-wide surveys to gain input. Others utilized small discussion groups, in which the objective was to gain honest response to the health and direction of the church, and to brainstorm new ideas.

Once again, a comparison of leaders at healthy and stagnant churches pinpoints the tenacious quest for quality as a major distinction between the two parties. In the growing churches, surveys were invariably used to provide insight. In some of the stagnant churches, when surveys were used, the purpose was more to confirm what the senior pastor believed than to open new windows of insight.

Indicative of this perspective were experiences in which the surveys were not allowed to include questions which gauged the performance of the senior pastor. "We don't need that information," one such pastor explained. He leads a church in southern California of several thousand people, although its numbers and community influence are waning. "I get enough feedback from my people that I know exactly how I'm doing. Besides, it wouldn't be meaningful for people who have no training to be passing judgment on my ability to teach them. My teaching style would not change, no matter what they said."

TAKING INVENTORY

Every successful church had some formal type of review session on Monday (or Tuesday), to assess every aspect of the Sunday experience. These people were serious about quality. They became upset when the same glitches occurred more than once or twice. They set high standards and made every effort to live up to those expectations.

Does your church have definable standards? How does your church measure how well it meets those standards? How frequently—and seriously—is the performance of the staff reviewed?

If you choose to pursue numerical growth, how will you protect your church from doctrinal compromise? Instituting safe-
guards against allowing minor, seemingly harmless decisions
that nevertheless water down your beliefs is best done before the
pursuit of growth begins.

When the church's ministry falters, is the church leadership
tightly-knit enough to acknowledge its failures? Is the response
one of shame and guilt, often leading to cover-ups, or one of
urgency to fix the problem so that ministry can be enhanced?
At user friendly churches, ministry was a team or family effort.
They knew that each individual or ministry would have off
days. But they also worked vehemently to overcome those
shortfalls, and to support each other during trying times. They
had learned to admit and confront failure, rather than sweep
those failures under the rug and continue to commit the same
mistakes.

5 THE CHURCH BEYOND SUNDAY

IF YOU HAD A DOLLAR FOR EVERY AMERICAN WHO THINKS THAT TAKING advantage of everything a church has to offer means attending the Sunday morning services, you'd be a wealthy person. For most people, "church" both describes a place and a Sunday morning activity. Sunday noon means freedom from further religious obligations until the next Sunday arrives.

But for many who belong to the successful churches I surveyed, "church" was more than just an occasional experience; it was a *life-style*. Being part of the church meant more than simply attending a weekly worship service. To some people it meant attending other events held during the week. To most, it had more to do with commitment to personal spiritual growth, through private or corporate activities such as prayer and Bible reading. Often, it also meant the ongoing pursuit of a changed life-style, and sharing their faith with other people.

Individuals who became regulars at successful churches understood that real Christianity is not a spectator sport. It is a participatory, hands-on way of life. They were compelled by calling and desire, rather than ritualistic obligation, to play a role in the work of the church. They recognized that just being in the right place at the appointed time was an empty demonstration of obedience that lacked meaning. Their goal was to *be* Christian by living in accordance with the principles Christ taught. They strove to *be the church*, at all times, in all places.

SECOND MILE MOTIVATION

What motivated these people to break from the typical behavior of their peers, to accept such an unusual and demanding form of commitment and to participate in activities to an extent that was clearly above the norm? My observations indicate that there were five underlying factors.

Teaching. The teachers at these churches, whether they were delivering a sermon or a class presentation, uniformly taught that every believer is to be a minister and thus must be in the world, doing ministry. One indicator used by these churches of the value of a person's teaching was evidence suggesting that the teaching was translated into practical ministry by those being taught. There was not much interest in these churches in providing teaching for the sake of teaching, or teaching which produced head knowledge but no ministry response.

Equipping. These churches devoted their resources to preparing the people for the work of the ministry. Times spent together were times to celebrate, worship, encourage and train. The efforts of church leaders were designed to prepare each individual to minister on behalf of Christ once they left the church campus.

Reinforcement. When people from the church were engaged in ministry, the Body felt a responsibility to commend their dedication to the cause, and to encourage them to continue doing such outreach. Because the people to whom those individuals were ministering were not likely to provide the kind of positive feedback necessary to maintain the high level of motivation and involvement deemed desirable, the church assumed that function through its corporate gatherings.

Modeling. The church would share examples of individuals

In all of the growing churches studied, efforts were made to remind people that their responsibility was to be the church, not just to attend one.

who were involved in ministry and making a difference in people's lives. Allowing the congregation to know that successful ministry is possible even in a hostile environment, and offering perspective on the contours of that ministry, helped to strengthen people's resolve to continue in their own ministry and to seek ways to upgrade their efforts. They were sensitive to the tension between putting a person on a pedestal to receive praise and making sure that the praise for a person's efforts was given to the Lord. The individual was the servant, the Lord was the Master; yet, there was a special joy taken in applauding the efforts of those who had been good and faithful servants.

Relevance. The church must consistently explore, describe and demonstrate the relevance of the Christian faith for people. Unless adults understand in very real ways how and why Christianity is meaningful to life today, they will not make the kind of commitment that the faith requires.

Naturally, not every person who attended the user friendly church adopted this radical perspective on the meaning of "church." However, in the typical successful church, a greater proportion of people than usual were committed to transforming their lives so that they *were* the church—living proof of the practicality of the gospel. Often, it seemed, the transformation that took place among the people of a successful church was as much a result of this attitude and life-style rubbing off from one person to another, as it was attributable to the teaching from the pulpit.

In all of the growing churches studied, efforts were made to remind people that their responsibility was to *be* the church, not just to *attend* one. Each of the pastors sought to prepare the congregation to take what happened in the sanctuary and on the church campus on Sundays into the marketplace on Monday through Saturday. They measured their own success as a leader of the congregation partly in accordance with how adequately their people lived out the Christian experience.

TAKING INVENTORY

When people leave the church after your services on Sunday, do they feel a sense of relief, as though they now have received their weekly dose of religion, and can get on with life? In user friendly churches, the attitude was one of expectancy. They anticipated being strengthened for the ensuing battle and being encouraged by the strength of their numbers and mutual dedication to the cause. Do the people in your congregation see themselves as part of a family that is united at least once a week for preparation, refreshment and encouragement?

What does your church do that makes Christianity relevant for those who attend? Relevance was a key word in the minds, speech and practices of each pastor connected to a growing church. This insistence upon relevance was precisely because they knew that today's adults (and youth, too) have so many alternatives to church. A church trying to compete for people's time and attention without providing a relevant ministry may as well not exist. They were also emphatic that the gospel is relevant to the very struggles and issues that fill the evening news and which throb in the minds of Americans. These pastors were passionate in describing how the gospel can be made the blueprint to meaningful response in the marketplace.

Who is in charge of monitoring, evaluating and coordinating the content of the teaching that takes place within your church? If you really want to energize people for ministry, the entire scope of the teaching transmitted within your congregation must be funneled through the same vision for education. Does every teacher—Sunday School, youth groups, small groups— understand what it means to make her or his teaching practical and relevant, toward equipping people for ministry?

6 EXPOSING THE SACRED COWS

A GOOD FRIEND OF MINE WAS A PRODUCER OF A PRIME-TIME TELEVISION program. The show received much fanfare, and had one of the highest production budgets in the industry. The best creative talent was hired, and the program drew a substantial audience its first week on the air.

Unfortunately, the executive producer of the show, who was financing the production, decided to award his wife one of the leading roles. While the woman had some talent and experience, she was indisputably wrong for the role. But her husband's desire for her career to take off, and his belief that her talent would prove itself to viewers, made it impossible for him to see the role mismatch. Even the pleas of his most trusted production advisors fell on deaf ears. He was determined that viewers would love both his show and his wife.

After an eight-week trial, the program was cancelled. Was is solely due to the fact that the producer's wife was undermining a critical part of the story with her amateurish acting? No. However, it certainly made it easier for audiences to criticize the show and tune it out. They could see that one of the pivotal roles was woefully miscast. With a myriad of viewing choices, viewers rejected the new program in favor of others that had ruthlessly examined themselves and done everything possible to enhance their performance.

AN EYE ON EXCELLENCE NOT PROTECTIONISM

In most of the churches I've worked with or studied that have plateaued or are in decline, certain aspects of the church's ministry are off-limits for review or discussion. Perhaps it is the quality of the pastor's preaching. Maybe it is the appearance of the buildings and grounds. In some cases it is the nature of the worship service, or the productivity of the staff. One church I worked with was very protective of the pastor's wife, who was responsible for the Christian education program in spite of her obvious lack of talent in that area.

Why worry about such protectionism? Simply put, the unwillingness to subject every element of the ministry to a fair and constructive evaluation process, which may result in change, means that the church is susceptible to deterioration due to negligence. That church cannot be completely serious about excellence; it must hold other goals in higher regard, or it would submit each aspect of the ministry to a reasonable examination by people whose purpose is to guard the health of the church.

Evaluation, Not Insulation

The successful churches we studied had no sacred cows. That is, everything about them was open to scrutiny and criticism. There were, of course, some boundaries as to how evaluations were conducted, and how any criticism was communicated. But there were no people, programs, facilities or ideas that were insulated from a fair and purposeful evaluation.

One of the interesting things about these churches was that they possessed a keen sense of ministry purpose, yet were willing to ask whether or not the church itself was still called to exist in that particular place, at that time, in its current form .

Questioning whether or not the church was a viable ministry was not seen as a threat, but as a means of remaining effective and in concert with God's plan for the church.

It is not uncommon for churches to have a process for evaluating the ministry. It is uncommon, however, for churches to subject the ministries and the people being evaluated to exacting scrutiny. There is often a concern that somebody's feelings might get hurt, or that someone might hold a grudge if a negative review is given. The implication of this approach, of course, is that it would be better to protect the feelings or the job of someone engaged in inferior ministry than to upgrade the ministry.

At the growing churches, people who had positions of responsibility in the Body (clergy and laity) did not feel threatened by the possibility that perhaps the time had come for the church to change some of its methods or personnel. They believed that if God had ordained the church to change functions or even to close its doors, He would also provide the wisdom for making those transitions. For staff members, this meant that they were confident that the Lord would not simply boot them out of a position, but would faithfully provide new and exciting ministry opportunities as well.

Change for the Positive

Having spent time talking with pastors about the anxiety that such evaluations can create, especially among full-time ministry personnel, I've come to believe that the ease with which clergy and staff at the growing churches accept the potential for such change is related to their belief in themselves. They initially obtained the position at the church because they were very competent at what they do. In most cases, that competence does not deteriorate.

Thus, the prospect of their being left jobless and hopeless, perhaps with a family to support, was not a cause of underlying anxiety. If a problem arose, and they were forced to leave the church, they were confident in their own abilities, and confident that God would choose to use those abilities in yet another situation.

Actually, there was little staff turnover in the growing churches. The issue of change rarely related to personnel as much as to programs. These churches consistently explored how well a program or project fit within the ministry vision of the church, and how closely it met the standards of the church.

The underlying objective of such explorations was to be certain that the church was optimizing its opportunities and minimizing the impact of its weaknesses. Because quality and purpose were so critical to the conduct and productivity of the church, such assessments were not seen as threats, but as a regular and necessary course of action to keep the church on track.

One strategy that helped these churches root out problems was the regularity of the evaluation process. In addition to addressing concerns at the time they emerged, these churches had a schedule on which a systematic evaluation occurred. This ensured leaders that no matter how out-of-control things got in a particular area of ministry, that problem would not exist for long. The regularity of the evaluation periods varied from church to church: some had a monthly evaluation session, in which a rotating schedule of ministries were examined. Others had a comprehensive review each quarter. None of the churches let any ministry or minister continue without at least an annual review; and even those churches that had an annual cycle incorporated periodic "quick checks" of the programs and personnel to be sure that things were performing well.

METHODS OF EVALUATION

A number of different methods of evaluation were utilized by churches. In some, outside consultants were hired to provide an expert eye. In others, the pastoral staff assumed the respon-

The unwillingness to sub-
ject...ministry to fair and
constructive evaluation...
means that the church is susceptible to deterioration due
to negligence.

sibility. In a few of the growing churches, a team of lay leaders, representing disparate factions of the congregation, were charged with the task of evaluation. In a few of the mainline churches, the governmental bodies (e.g. deacons, elders) were responsible. Regardless of who comprised the evaluation group, the call to action was the same across churches: be fair, thorough, honest and quick.

Quick evaluations were another distinction between growing and stagnant churches. In growing churches, the emphasis was upon ministry, not upon meetings and administrative tasks. The growing churches realized the importance of doing everything well. But they also acknowledged that taking time out from "real ministry" to evaluate the conduct of various ministries was a sacrifice. It also had the potential to be intrusive for the ministries being examined. The procedures employed, therefore, were meant to be quick and painless, though insightful.

One crucial factor that allowed the process to work smoothly was the existence of well-defined goals and plans for each ministry. While the growing churches were not heavily weighed down by paperwork requirements, they did mandate that each staff member and program leader provide some written goals for their ministry within the coming period. Without such goals, an evaluation could easily turn into a subjective battle of personalities and personal preferences. When the evaluation had some objective mileposts to be compared with, the procedures were facilitated.

Another tangible difference between the growing and stagnant churches is that the leaders of growing churches believed that no matter how well a program was working, or how strong the results of a particular ministry were, those results could be improved or enhanced. They were rarely willing to settle for a particular level of performance. They knew that the environment in which they were ministering was both changing and challenging. They understood that outsiders or visitors were often skeptical. They were dedicated to finding and remaining on the cutting edge of meeting people's most acute needs. They attempted to walk the fine line between being picky and being constructive. Criticism for the sake of criticism found little appreciation in these churches.

TAKING INVENTORY

What ministry activities are considered out-of-bounds for discussion or scrutiny at your church? Perhaps there are some good reasons for not permitting study of those people or programs. What are those reasons?

How often does the church go over every element of the church with a fine-tooth comb, willing to admit that some areas of outreach or perspective need to be reassessed and sharpened? In successful churches, not only is there an informal, consistent evaluation underway at all times; there are formal times designed for evaluating what the church does. Perhaps your church could be propelled forward by establishing more regularity in its review procedures.

When feedback is garnered, is it simply coming from the staff and a few lay leaders, or is it from a broader, more objective base? In user friendly churches, efforts are made to include the opinions and perceptions of newcomers and veterans, people who have been on the inside of the church's leadership and those who have no idea what it takes to make the church tick. The aim is to have the benefit of a cross-section of ideas and input in order to better understand whether the church's ministry is real and significant. How does your church gather and analyze the opinions and perceptions of the "average" member and visitor?

Are there areas of ministry for which your church is especially proud or best-known? Sometimes it is those areas of pride which may become the foundation of your downfall. Without a consistent review of how well those ministries are doing, and how adequately they are adapting to the constantly shifting needs of those being ministered to, it is very possible that over time the "showcase ministries" of the church will become ineffective, or even embarrassments.

SECTION II

PARTICIPATION AND PROGRAMS

You are a chosen people, a royal priesthood, a holy nation, a people belonging to God, that you may declare the praises of him who called you out of darkness into his wonderful light. . . . Live such good lives among the pagans that, though they accuse you of doing wrong, they may see your good deeds and glorify God on the day he visits us (1 Pet. 2:9, 12).

IN EVALUATING WHAT MADE CHURCHES SUCCESSFUL, IT BECAME apparent that the behavior of people in growing churches is different from the behavior of people in stagnant or declining churches. When it comes to observing the activities in which people participate, and how they conduct themselves in those activities, "If you've seen one, you've seen them all" does *not* accurately describe the lives of churches.

A major difference is that people in user friendly churches were active participants in the church's ministry. They did not divorce their faith from their life-style; their faith *was* their lifestyle. They took seriously the classical Reformation doctrine of the priesthood of all believers. In stagnant churches, the laity were more likely to be observers than participants. They perceived their role as being an audience in the stands, nodding approvingly as the clergy went through their paces in efforts to demonstrate religious behavior.

Growing churches consistently practiced what they preached. The people who comprised their congregations were not the least bit self-conscious about their behavior. That is, they were not anxious about being on display, and having to put on a worthy exhibition. Yes, they were aware that a Christian may be held to a higher standard "among the pagans" or in the marketplace, and is at any given moment being evaluated by nonbelievers. However, the beliefs and actions most consistent with Christianity had become ingrained for many of these people. They ceased to see a dichotomy between their Christian life and their normal life.

When it came to taking part in church-oriented activities, the laity participated because they wanted to and because they were genuinely excited about the potential results. It was that excitement about the potential outcome of their ministry-mindedness that motivated their behavior. It is that behavior which we will examine in the following five chapters.

Keep in mind that behavior helps us understand priorities. Most people devote their time, money and energy to those matters which they consider to be most important. It seems that the people who comprise these churches have a similar set of priorities, as defined by common behavior. ➡

7 | THE MASTER'S PLAN FOR YOUR CHURCH

ISN'T IT INTERESTING THAT WE HAVE NO PROBLEM ASSURING PEOPLE that God has a plan for each person's life, but we rarely take seriously the notion that He also has a precise plan for each *church* He has ordained to exist?

People in the churches I surveyed seemed to apply to their own church God's promise to Israel, through Jeremiah:

"'I will come to you and fulfill my gracious promise . . . . For I know the plans I have for you,' declares the LORD, 'plans to prosper you and not to harm you, plans to give you hope and a future'" (Jer. 29:10, 11).

GOD'S VISION FOR YOUR CHURCH

At each successful church, there was a clear understanding of God's plans to give the church a hope and a future. It was not perceived to be the vision of the pastor, or of a strategic planning committee or one promoted by the denomination. It was understood as *God's* vision for the church. There is a huge difference between God's vision for us and the ideas we dream up on our own.

How did these churches arrive at an understanding of what

God had in store for them? Through significant amounts of study, prayer and counsel. The importance of this step cannot be overestimated: it may be the single most important corner-stone of a successful, Bible-based ministry. The leaders of the churches studied concurred that unless they were driven by God's vision, they were bound to fail. Once in tune with the vision, it became the call to action that motivated clergy and laity alike. That vision became the filter through which all church activities were evaluated. Activities which coincided with the vision were pursued, and those which fell outside the parameters of the vision were rejected.

During my evaluation, I witnessed one church which turned down the chance to host a world-renowned choir visiting from another country. The promoters of the choir spent thousands of advertising dollars for each of its limited engagements, and thousands of people were attracted to the host church. Yet, with-in an hour of the offer, the pastor contacted the choir to polite-ly turn down the offer.

The pastor explained to me that while the offer was flatter-ing, the style of music would attract a different audience than that to which the church was geared to minister. Hosting the choir would send a conflicting signal to people about the church and its mission. Although he received flack from his denomi-nation and even from some members of the church (apparent-ly not everyone understood the vision), he, his staff and his lay leadership team were very comfortable with the decision, and gave no signs of second guessing it.

Owning the Vision

In each successful church, an interesting phenomenon was observed: passion for the vision was handed down from the top of the church leadership ladder. Unless the senior pastor, the associate pastors and the staff were fully behind the vision, the chances of creating a congregation that passionately follows was diminished. In fact, the vision invariably started with the

Ministry vision was not to be a jealously hoarded secret....In all the growing churches studied, the average member was able to articulate the church's vision.

pastor. He then communicated it to the staff, who in turn shared it with the lay leadership. Ultimately, all three levels of leaders did their part to share the vision with the church at large.

In like manner, one of the most crucial responsibilities of each individual in the church was to catch the vision and transfer it to others. If only the leaders possessed the vision, and it was not passed on to the body, that ministry would have little chance of success. The ministry vision was not to be a jealously hoarded secret, but a perspective to be communicated with excitement and fervor. Vision only bore fruit when it was shared among, and embraced by, the body.

Articulating the Vision

In all of the growing churches studied, the average member was able to articulate the vision. Although each person might use different words, different examples and even different applications, the vision's description was essentially the same.

In successful churches, people were encouraged to articulate the vision through life-style, not just the repetition of the right words. While the degree of emphasis placed upon this type of commitment varied from church to church, all of the growing churches clearly believed that behavioral modeling was the most effective means of communicating a concept to people outside the church. Thus, a vision that did not translate into overt action by the people was a vision that had little real support and ownership. Lacking such support and ownership, the vision—and probably the church—would fail to grow.

Focusing the Vision

This understanding, and the ability to communicate a clear direction and purpose, was the result of a church that was focused. Its attention and energy were concentrated on a specific goal that it believed God had commissioned it to accomplish. At all times, the words and actions of the staff and leadership of the successful church reinforced the vision. Armed with this notion of calling by God, the church could cheerfully admit that it could not possibly be all things to all people and hope to minister with power and excellence. Successful churches acknowledged that they would dilute their impact by trying to cover all the bases; being spread too thin was not a virtue. (See chapters 3 and 8 for more about this aspect.)

These churches also recognized that a vision from God must be precise. "To lead souls to Christ" or "to help those in need" are not vision statements, but rather affirmations of a desire to be involved in ministry. Those are very broad statements about ministry that do not really help people understand the direction of the church or the uniqueness of its vision.

Successful churches composed vision statements that defined specific target audiences and missions that would serve as the focus of the aggregate church outreach.

Successful churches also recognized the risk of limiting an individual's vision for personal ministry by the description of the church's corporate vision. Church leaders were careful not to undermine the perceived ministry of an individual when it was different from the focus of the church at large. Individuals were encouraged to fulfill the vision for ministry that God had given to them, and to seek creative ways in which that outreach might be done in cooperation with what the church was doing.

Transmitting the Vision

But with both visitors and members attending all at once, how does the church's vision get transmitted and reinforced to the church's faithful, without turning off those who are simply observing?

The turning point is when an individual makes a commitment to the church. This may be when a person applies for formal membership, or asks how to become more involved in the outreach of the church. The keys to the process are that the individual, not the church, makes the first move; and that the church responds to the person's interest by clearly explaining why the church exists, and the role of the participant within the scope of the vision.

Churches used various means of guiding the inquiring individual into a deeper relationship with the church. In most churches, interested people were asked to attend an enquirer's class. In other cases, they were invited to spend an evening, over dinner, with a key leader in the church, discussing relevant matters. In a few of the churches, a series of audio- and videotapes were used in conjunction with written materials which provided deeper information.

HE WHO HAS EARS TO HEAR

Persuasive communication can occur only when the party to be persuaded has an interest in what the persuader has to say. In the case of a church, this interest is signalled when a person asks for an explanation of the church's mission, or how to play a larger role in that mission. It is at that point that an explanation of the vision for ministry will have the greatest potential to penetrate the individual's consciousness. To try to impress the person with the vision before they are interested generally has little impact. But once a person is ready to hear, a precise declaration of why God has called that church into existence is merited, and stands the best chance of hitting home.

If an individual chooses to make an even deeper commitment to the Body (e.g., formal membership, volunteer), this provides the church with yet another opportunity to explain what it is about. When the individual expresses an interest in participating in the ministry, the successful church takes the opportunity to first describe what the church's ministry is, explaining the vision in practical terms. In other words, people who want to be part of the church have to understand the church, which means comprehending and owning the vision.

One of the churches, a mainline congregation in the midwest, found that before it had articulated a clear and precise statement of vision for ministry, the congregation had no sense of direction, and little felt need to become involved in church activity. Once the vision was articulated—through a letter sent to all parishioners, a sermon on the meaning of the vision for ministry, and a special series of midweek classes on the integration of the vision with the outreach activities of the church—people began to see that they could enter an entirely new realm of spiritual endeavor and growth. Members became excited about the potential for the future. They began inviting friends to experience the renewed congregation, and serious outreach programs of all types began to flourish.

TAKING INVENTORY

As a leader in your church, can you articulate God's vision for your church right now, in one or two sentences? If it takes more than two sentences, it may not be clear or succinct enough for people to grab onto and own. And if you cannot articulate the vision, chances are good that most others in the church cannot do so, either.

Is your vision specific enough that it will allow you to say no to certain ministry opportunities? A common vision statement is "to reach the world for Christ" or "to win the lost to Christ" or some similar statement. While this is nice, it is not a statement of vision; it is a definition of ministry. Your vision statement should be stated with precision, and should therefore enable you to evaluate how various ministry options fit in with the church's reason for being. If your vision statement does not point you in a very specific direction and allow you to say no to some of the many opportunities you will encounter, you probably need to reexamine its clarity and scope. A vision that is too broad is tantamount to no vision at all.

When do people hear and see the vision articulated? Does your church have a conscious and well-conceived strategy for communicating the vision to those who wish to become part of the Body? Successful churches have worked through how they will pass on the vision to others. Among the strategies used were:

- devoting a significant portion of the new member class to a detailed explanation of the vision;
- preaching an annual sermon devoted to restating the vision, and tying it to the goals and programs of the church;
- placing a statement of the vision in high profile church publications, such as the weekly bulletin, newsletter or other member communication vehicle;
- providing an audiotape of the vision, explained by the pastor, to all who were involved in the church;
- having every ministry leader (elders, deacons, chairpersons of ministry teams) include with any request for new resources (money, time, labor, materials) a justification based upon the meshing of the activity with the vision.

Make sure that you have developed a strategy for integrating the vision into all endeavors of your church. To allow activity to happen without such a check is to invite disaster.

Some churches convey conflicting messages about the significance of the vision by allocating resources to church ministries that are not in tune with the vision. While many of these ministries may be worthy of support, if they do not fit snugly within the parameters of what the church has been called to do, as expressed within God's vision for the church, it is probably counterproductive to support such outreach. This is a hard lesson for many churches to learn. Does your church support efforts that are outside the boundaries of its vision?

If the people of your congregation were asked to rate the passion of the senior pastor and the staff about the church's vision, where would they rate on a scale of 1 to 100? Remember, if you expect busy, skilled, intelligent people to accept the vision, they must be convinced that it is worth accepting. If you wish to gain widespread acceptance of the vision, your people must believe that you and other key leaders in the church are 100 percent behind the vision, and wholly focused on its implementation. If your church is to grow, such widespread acceptance is nonnegotiable. It *must* happen.

8 EVERYONE'S A MARKETER

IMAGINE WHAT IT MUST BE LIKE, BEING THE PASTOR OF A CHURCH OF 5,000 people and knowing with certainty that this year your church will gain at least 500 new active participants—without your having to invest much personal energy in identifying and inviting those people.

That's exactly the scenario that characterized the growing churches studied for this book. How did they do it?

The key was that the people who were members or regular attenders of the churches consistently invited other people with whom they had built relationships to attend the church. This is all the more remarkable since we live in an age when such boldness is unusual and unexpected.

PORTRAIT OF A MARKETER

Research consistently demonstrated that visitors came to these churches because of the recommendation, invitation or consistent attendance of a neighbor, friend or work associate. This corresponds with findings from national studies of church membership and attendance. People are most likely to visit churches which have been recommended by someone they trust.

People seeking a church to attend generally do not rely upon information provided in a newspaper advertisement or other form of mass communication. The suggestion of a trusted individual carries credibility that is rarely duplicated by other means of communication.

Why did the people of the growing churches invite their friends? A variety of reasons answer this question.

- Some felt that the church had helped them, and that it would likely provide the same type of assistance for others.
- Some said that the issues addressed by the church, the answers provided to those issues or the manner in which church activities were conducted were relevant to their own needs and interests.
- Other people said that the church reacted to them as mature adults, neither treating them like children nor badgering them with requests for untenable commitments.
- Some individuals were simply proud of their church, believing it was a place in which God was doing great things for all people, through His people.

The Pastor's Role

While it is true that the responsibility for attracting visitors was removed from the pastor, he did have a very special responsibility, of course. In every instance, the pastor was instrumental in instilling a new perspective in the minds of those in the congregation. In short, one of his tasks was to make everyone a marketer.

Realize, of course, that few pastors used the M-word ("marketing"). Often, the concept was cloaked in the Christian-speak we tend to use in our churches, making a potentially uncomfortable concept accessible and comfortable. Through teaching about the nature of the church, the faithful came to see that *they* were the evangelists called by God to bring others into a

It was not the task of a "visitation or evangelism team" to make the visitor feel welcome. The strategy called for the person who did the inviting to also provide on-site hospitality and post-visit debriefing.

meaningful relationship with Him. They saw a critical part of their role within the church to be the planting of spiritual seeds in people's lives, seeds that might become fruitful with further nurturing. They caught that part of the vision of the church which described them as life-style evangelists.

The Members' Role

Further, at these user friendly churches, members realized that inviting people to church was only part of their responsibility. The inviters acknowledged that they also were responsible for accompanying the guest to the church activity, as well as for following up with them. It was not the task of a "visitation team" or an "evangelism team" to make the visitor feel welcome. The strategy called for the person who did the inviting to also provide the on-site hospitality and the post-visit debriefing.

The follow-up was handled in different ways by different churches, but it always relied upon the inviter to take the responsibility. In some churches, the follow-up was done immediately after the worship service (e.g., taking the guest out to brunch, and discussing the experience or answering any questions). In other churches, the follow-up was expected to occur at some time during the six days following the service, in the normal course of conversation or other interaction. It was well understood that the church might send a thank-you note to visitors, but that such correspondence was *not* intended to substitute for the warm, personal contact that had encouraged the visitor to give the church a try in the first place.

This perspective of making the host responsible for follow-up is a major point of distinction from most churches that actively pursue guests. A church in California which is struggling to grow hasn't caught on yet that although it attracts an ample number of visitors, less than 10 percent return. Why? Because the people who invite those people are either too scared, too busy or too unaware to interact with the guest about their experience. They send an evangelism team to visit the guest. Their records reflect that increasing numbers of people will not allow the team in the house, and among those who allow entry, there are few positive results. Why? Those intruders have no relationship, and therefore no credibility, with the visitors.

In several of the communities in which the growing churches were located, I also found that even people who were not members or regular attenders of the church recommended the church to their friends or to new residents. It seems that the church had built such a strong level of awareness within the community, and had such a positive image, that even the people who did not personally feel the need to attend regularly felt comfortable enough with the church to suggest it to those who inquired.

The long-term benefit is that when these people are ready to return to a church, the first place they are likely to go is the very place that they recommended to others. In its own way, this reflected the successful planting of seeds in the lives of those people who were difficult to get into a church for any reason.

One of the churches had so adeptly created the image of being a warm, community-based church that when it was time to obtain a building permit for new construction, the process was facilitated by the fact that members of the zoning board (none of whom attended the church) knew that the congregation was doing very positive and beneficial things within the community. They were aware of those activities because friends of theirs did attend the church, and consistently invited them to those community events.

The A-Word

Did these successful churches use traditional advertising? To some extent, yes. Their budgets, however, for newspaper advertising, radio commercials, direct mail and other forms of mass communication were relatively limited. One church with an $8 million annual budget was spending less than $20,000 on advertising, but still realizing 14 percent annual growth in attendance.

In fact, the advertising money of the churches under study was spent for a different purpose than usual. Most churches advertise to gain "new customers"—that is, to persuade people of the merits of their "product." In the growing churches, though, advertising tended to be *informative* rather than *persuasive*. Because they were relying upon a different medium (word-of-mouth) to achieve persuasion, they used traditional forms of advertising primarily to build awareness.

This is sound practice. Before people will visit a church, they must first know the church exists, then become knowledgeable about what it is all about and finally attain a positive impression of the church. This opens the way to considering attending the church. By providing this sound bedrock of information through traditional advertising, the task of the church member who invites an individual to attend is greatly simplified.

TAKING INVENTORY

Does your church advertise through the media or via direct marketing methods (mailings, telemarketing, etc.)? If so, what are you trying to achieve through your advertising? If you are using advertising in an attempt to persuade people to attend the church, know that you will need a hefty advertising budget, a clever strategy and superb creative execution to penetrate people's consciousness.

Even if you rely upon media to attract people to the church, realize that how your people respond to those visitors will be a key to determining whether or not the visitors will return. Think through how your people fit into the marketing activity of your church. Do not ignore them as a resource. Overall, they are your most effective and efficient marketing tool.

How do you measure the effectiveness of your advertising? A major mistake of most American churches is to spend money on advertising without a way to ascertain whether or not the expenditure was worthwhile. Before you budget funds for advertising, be sure that you have some reasonable means of determining what type of return you receive from your investment.

If the people in your church do not invite their friends and associates to your church, find out why. You may discover that they have not caught your vision for ministry, or that they do not understand the member-as-evangelist strategy. It could be that your people lack sufficient pride in the church to invite their friends. This latter issue is indicative of a deeper, more serious problem: an ineffective ministry which may also result in the poor retention of existing members. Detecting this difficulty—or any of the other shortcomings associated with people's refusal to invite friends—must be remedied quickly.

A common problem among Christians is that once they find Christ and become involved in the church, they begin to lose contact with people who are outside of the church. This is both natural and dangerous. It is dangerous because we then begin to lose opportunities to build the very relationships with the unchurched or with nonbelievers (many of whom may be churched) which enable us to invite them to attend our church. What are you, as a church leader, doing to prevent this ingrown tendency? Do you have a consistent number of relationships with people from outside the body? Are individuals in your congregation encouraged to maintain such relationships? Does your church have any strategies to prevent your people from becoming isolated from non-Christians or from the unchurched?

Another frequent difficulty I've seen is churches failing to equip people to do the necessary follow-up. How sad it is to witness Christians who sincerely want to impact people, but are not prepared for the task. In America today, adults are amazingly inept not only at building relationships, but at nurturing them. We have generally lost the ability to communicate effectively with each other. Christians, in particular, struggle with this dilemma. When placed in an evangelistic situation, they frequently come on too strong, and lose much of the credibility they had sought to build in their relationships.

Has your church prepared its people to deal with visitors after an experience at the church? Growing churches learned—the hard way, in several cases—that they had to teach people how to converse about the visitor's experience. One church has a seminar on how to build and maintain relationships with nonchurch people. Another church incorporates a discussion of such skills into a pair of sermons given annually by the preacher. In one congregation, such information is disseminated through the small group studies arranged through the church. Yet another of the growing churches has a special dramatic presentation in which it depicts what it's like for a visitor to attend the church, and what it's like for a host to have the visitor present—and scenarios of what happens after the visit.

Finally, remember that while church growth might emphasize the attraction of new people to the congregation, it is critically important to retain individuals who are already part of the congregation. How does your church make sure that the people who comprise your core membership are being connected with each other? What mechanisms have been developed to ascertain how well the church is bringing people together in relationships? Is somebody responsible for keeping track of the health of the relationships that form the foundation of the church itself?

9 GROW OR GO

For someone who has been a part of a stagnant church, or who has been away from church altogether, attending a healthy, aggressive church can be very challenging. Interviews with those people indicated that upon visiting such a church they were immediately impressed with a different mentality from what they expected. They sensed very quickly that the people who were regulars at the church were not playing the typical Sunday morning game. Being at church was not a routine, a series of rote actions performed on cue. Coming together for a worship experience on Sunday, or some other type of experience on other days of the week, was something they clearly enjoyed, something they looked forward to. It was an act of passion.

The difference visitors sensed was related to the fine-tuned sense of purpose maintained by members of the user friendly churches. They attended church events and services because they believed their attendance would bear fruit in their own lives. Experience had taught them that of the two choices they had—to attend or not attend—they would be more likely to grow spiritually by being involved in what the church had to offer.

In most stagnant churches, people attend programs, events

and activities for reasons that often smack of duty, obligation or social contact, rather than earnest desire or interest. Whether the pressure was a result of family expectations, a sense of guilt or the desirability of being seen by others in a church setting, the result was often a hollow victory, if a victory at all.

Individuals involved with the user friendly churches saw attendance at the church events, programs and activities as compelling. They freely committed their time because they believed they would emerge as better people. The church did not have to beg people to turn out for upcoming events. People came because they believed they would miss something valuable if they did not attend.

I was particularly fascinated by the behavior of the people at a fundamentalist church we studied. The church had a very extensive program of services and activities in which people could engage. What was surprising was how fervently people evaluated those options. When filling in their personal calendars, these people tended to schedule church activities first, then fill in the gaps with other, outside alternatives of interest.

REASONS FOR LIFE-STYLE COMMITMENT

Why is there such a difference between the growing churches I studied and the typical stagnant church?

For one thing, people attending growing churches were more likely to have their expectation of *high quality* in ministry satisfied. Like most Americans, people in these churches have high expectations in general—and at church they got what they expected. In fact, they were trained to accept nothing less.

Also, people involved with growing churches were more likely to have their felt needs ministered to through the efforts of the church. Growing churches offered people a top-notch ministry that addressed the most important issues with which they were struggling. It was this felt-needs approach to ministry that caused people to return, week after week, in spite of the lofty odds against doing so.

The Felt-Needs Approach

There has been increasing talk in pastoral circles about the dangers of "pandering to people's felt needs." The fear is that by paying attention to what people feel they need, we will remove our focus from the essence of the gospel and begin to compromise the message of Christ.

These healthy and growing churches proved that this need not be the case. They did not view a needs-oriented ministry as a marketing gimmick, but as a method of ensuring effective ministry. Several of the pastors had learned from prior experience that without a felt-needs approach, creating spiritual growth in the membership was often extremely slow, if not impossible. Instead, they saw a needs-based outreach as a way of plowing the fertile fields. Knowing what was on people's minds, and applying the truth of Scripture, guaranteed that they would have an attentive audience.

Adopting Christ's Perspective

Pastors of the user friendly churches tended to draw examples from the Bible of how Jesus utilized this approach in His ministry. The common approach was for Him to begin to build a relationship by focusing on the needs of the other person, addressing those needs with tangible assistance, then sharing with them the larger, more enduring principles that would be of the greatest help in the long-run. The significance of Christ's strategy is underscored by the fact that disciples such as Peter and Paul relied on the very same approach.

People want meaningful solutions to their deepest struggles. The church, if it is prepared, may have the opportunity to address those needs by applying the practicality and the truth of the gospel to those needs. By allowing the people themselves to dictate the path along which they would grow spiritually, and entrusting the means and integrity of that growth to the church leaders, everyone emerged a winner.

Many of the growing churches had their own bookstores or audiotape distribution centers. Their people were constantly seeking opportunities to gain practical insights into God's Word. They bought tapes, books and instructional materials in unprecedented quantities. And they frequently purchased the tape of the sermon they just listened to. Why? Because they felt that any resource that moved them closer to being more learned, more effective or better prepared Christians was a resource worth having. They treated their faith as a serious undertaking, and wanted to utilize those tools available to propel them forward along the track of wholeness.

A Hands-on Laity

Interestingly, the pastors of these churches indicated that the new ministry areas sponsored by the church were often the result of suggestions or requests from lay people. Rather than waiting for the church to initiate new and needed programs within the church or community, these people took it upon themselves to recommend needed ministries. Often, they also took the lead in the development and management of those ministries. (The pastors of several of these churches even went so far as to institute policies which mandated that any new ministry had to be initiated and managed by the laity, with staff acting as a resource.)

These active lay people, growing in the knowledge of their gifts, and being sensitized to the opportunities they had to reach a dying world, acted out of a sense of urgency. They hoped to influence others before it was too late, and they perceived time to be of the essence in ministry. To them, every day that passed represented one less day they had to share Christ with people who needed to hear the gospel.

The pastor of an evangelical Baptist church in Colorado noted that he had learned that if there was not enough interest

By allowing the people themselves to dictate the path along which they would grow spiritually, and entrusting the means and integrity of that growth to the church leaders, everyone emerged a winner.

on the part of the laity to support a "needed" ministry, then it wasn't really needed. He also described a system that had been developed for recommending a new area of ministry. After expressing the idea to a pastor, it was developed in a more formal program description; presented to a committee of church leaders; given approval, denial or ideas for redevelopment; and incorporated into the weekly church announcement of ministry opportunities and funding availability.

After more than a decade of refining this approach, the pastor also indicated that he felt his greatest responsibility in this area was to "give people permission to do ministry. The last thing they need is someone telling them that God does not really want them to use their gifts for touching the lives of other people." He has denied permission only in those cases of truly bizarre or unconscionable ministries (e.g., advocacy of "Christian" alcoholism).

User friendly churches were invariably congregations in which the people felt that they were associated with an organization that was really going somewhere. They sometimes struggled to keep up with the pace—but they generally felt that it was worth the effort.

Looking Outward

Sadly, in many churches people's attention is focused exclusively upon themselves. In the growing churches I studied there was, of course, some self-centeredness. However, there was a greater emphasis upon outreach than inreach. The people attending these churches were slowly but consistently stripped of their "me" focus and firmly led to focus upon Christ, through attention and service to other people. This was one of the healthiest aspects of these churches.

Our research shows that churches usually die from the inside out. Death is largely due to an inward focus, rather than an outward concern. The growing churches maintained the belief that to be the family of Christ they had to balance these competing perspectives. Often that meant addressing the needs of the "have nots"—whether what they did not have was a relationship with Jesus Christ, physical health, emotional wholeness or other desired aspects.

Again, the cues given by church leaders help to dictate the sincerity of the church in its efforts to grow via outreach. At one of the nondenominational churches, the pastor expressed great dismay when the fund drive for a building campaign exceeded its dollar goal by 35 percent. His dismay was based on the realization that relatively few people had provided the funding. This was taken as an indication that the leadership needed once again to retrench, and to help people to reevaluate their priorities and understand the role of stewardship in personal spiritual growth. The pastor's frustration had nothing to do with the amount of money given, but with the narrow base it represented and the unwillingness of so many to give. It was not an issue of finances, but an issue of the heart of the people toward ministry.

Missions as Mainstream

Not surprisingly, these churches had a greater sense of the importance of missions and outreach, and a deeper commitment to missions, than do most churches. In most cases, support for missions was such an accepted fact of life that "missions" ceased being a separate element of the overall ministry—it was just as much a part of the mainstream work of the church as music, prayer and worship.

Importantly, though, the growing churches were not content to let missions support simply relate to the giving of money. Through a wide range of opportunities, the churches encouraged people to give their time as well as their money. Some churches partnered with parachurch organizations to afford the opportunity to get involved: housing through Habitat for Humanity, minority education through Mendenhall Ministries, homeless relief in cooperation with local missions, and so forth.

Other congregations created their own programs to address priority issues. The pastors all agreed that appropriate involvement in missions is not to throw money at a group that does the work of missions, and then to forget about that effort. They sought an approach that not only ministered to those in need but also afforded members opportunities for personal growth. Thus they called the people to sacrifice the resources they covet the most: their time and their security.

Facilitators of Growth

A few of the pastors mentioned that their strategies for personal growth make many adults uncomfortable. Some even choose to leave the church once they discover the emphasis attached to consistent personal growth. The "grow or go" philosophy is too much for some people to bear. "And that's fine," one pastor explained. "There are plenty of churches where they can attend as spectators. In this church, Christianity is not a spectator sport. It's an active life-style. Stand still and you lose ground."

A final observation about the commitment to personal growth. Compared to the typical church, these churches made it easy for people to grow. They planned far enough ahead of time so that people could build their lives around what the church was doing. They remained so sensitive to the needs of the people that there was little anxiety over whether or not the church leadership could be trusted to provide valuable teaching, programs and other activities. And there was never any doubt about the underlying goal of the church, or the motives behind any new direction the church pursued.

TAKING INVENTORY

Has your church set high standards for performance in ministry, and set about to minister to people's felt needs? In today's society, commitment to satisfying felt needs through excellence in effort is the only sure ticket to growth. Each of the successful churches studied made a considerable and ongoing effort to remain abreast of the felt needs in the congregation and in the community. Their outreach was geared to satisfying people's hunger for understanding and support in those areas of need— and they did so without compromising the gospel. What can your church do to become better acquainted with people's needs? What can you do to enable the quality of ministry to *exceed* people's expectations, thereby encouraging them to return week after week?

You might also examine what your church does that effectively prevents people from growing. What activities have become so routine that they lack meaning or stifle excitement? Are there elements of your outreach that enable people to become so comfortable that they lose their interest in being stretched spiritually? After a period of rapid growth, churches sometimes need a brief period in which to stabilize, a time to catch their breath before charging ahead again. Unfortunately, that breather period sometimes becomes so prolonged that the church gets stuck in a relaxation mode, never to regain its sharp edge. Be diligent in objectively examining the vitality of your church. Stagnation is a painful way to die.

If the people in your community were asked who your church is most concerned about, what would their answer be? In too many instances, the response would be "themselves" or "the members of the church." To get beyond the country club mentality, help people understand that spiritual growth—either the maturing of the individual or of the congregation—is the result of achieving a balance between external and internal focus.

With the current emphasis on psychology, self-esteem and the search for emotional wholeness, we sometimes get side-tracked and dwell on our own needs, to the exclusion of the needs of others. Does your church have a well-balanced program of inreach and outreach, enabling members to mature in Christ?

Growing numbers of churches today are on the decline because they allow their people to concentrate on themselves, in the hope that these individuals will achieve personal wholeness and then feel released to focus on others. This process is self-defeating if the church allows its people to wait for perfection before concentrating on other people.

The churches studied for this book generally taught a divergent path to personal growth. They suggested that the best way to achieve self-growth was by focusing on others, not self. Rather than encouraging people to seek wholeness by making their own interests paramount, they taught the value of ministering to others as a means of ministering to self. What can you do to help your people recognize the opportunities for ministry to the community, and to live that mission as though it really counts?

How often do the people in your congregation read books about the Christian life, or study commentaries while reading the Bible? How frequently do they listen to tapes of great sermons, or to significant radio ministries? How often do the leaders of the church help the people identify available resources, and model the use of those resources in their own spiritual development? One of the great barriers to personal spiritual growth is people's ignorance of available tools. How tragic it is that many people are stuck in a spiritual rut simply because they have not been alerted to the range of growth resources available for their use.

10 YOU DO NOT HAVE BECAUSE YOU DO NOT ASK

AN ELDER IN A SMALL CHURCH WHOSE MINISTER HAD RESIGNED HAD been anxious about who the church should call to be its new pastor. A busy professional person, the elder was not given to spending much time in prayer. He was, instead, accustomed to deciding on a plan of action, and acting on the plan. Finally, after several months, a new minister accepted a call from the church. The elder was overjoyed at the way things had worked out despite his anxiety. He was also somewhat chagrined that he had not trusted God and prayed more during the process. It was only half-jokingly that he wisecracked: "As luck would have it, providence was with us!"

A CALL TO PRAYER

The elder may have just been more honest than many. In most churches, prayer has become something to which we pay lip service. We say we believe in it, but we rarely get beyond a recitation of form prayers or a barrage of requests that we want God to answer at His earliest convenience. And when things work out right, we are as likely to credit it to "luck" as to the providence of God.

As evidence of the tepid interest in prayer, notice that when voluntary, organized prayer activities are attempted they generally attract very small groups of people. In fact, few Protestant churches have any form of prayer ministry outside of the regularly-scheduled services and events.

Prayer was one of the foundation stones of ministry in the user friendly churches examined for this book. The call to prayer was the battle cry of the congregation: it rallied the troops. These people understood the power of prayer. They actively and consistently included prayer in their services, their events, their meetings and their personal ministries.

People in these churches were more likely than usual to view prayer as an opportunity to be in the presence of God, and to be filled with His mind. They were more likely than usual to insist that prayer be a central part of any decisions made by the church. They typically perceived prayer to be a two-way conversation, in which listening was every bit as important as talking.

How did this condition come about? It was the result of a four-part emphasis upon prayer.

1. *The congregation was exposed to biblical teaching about the role of prayer in the Christian life.* Prayer was described in its totality, in order to equip people with the understanding and skills to make prayer an integral part of their spiritual life. The ways in which prayer was taught varied, from imploring people to remember acrostics that would help them recall the elements of prayer (e.g., ACTS—acknowledgment, confession, thanksgiving, supplication) to detailed Bible studies in which people would be taught prayer forms. The consistent reality was that in each church, people regularly heard about the importance and the methods of prayer from the pulpit and through other educational forums connected with the church.

2. *Church leaders (staff and laity) modeled prayer as normal and significant behavior in all aspects of the Christian life.* The pastors of these growing churches made it clear, through intimate conversations with people about spiritual

Prayer was never short-changed. Several pastors indicated that they would rather reduce the time allotted to their sermons than to minimize or abbreviate the time in which the congregation was in conversation with God.

character and development as well as by their daily behavior, that prayer was not an option but a necessity. These people were comfortable with prayer; their first thought, when faced with a decision or problem, was to go to the Lord in prayer; and descriptions of progress in their personal life always touched on involving prayer as an integral element in that progress.

I was impressed by the thoughtful reflection of these men regarding the power of prayer in their ministries. One pastor, known for his powerful preaching, indicated that he spends more time in prayer about his sermon than he does in preparing his notes. Another minister produced a journal in which he had catalogued his prayers over the past year, and how God had revealed answers through prayer and meditation.

Yet another pastor, when asked what differentiated his church from others that were not having the impact of his church, responded: "Prayer. We believe in prayer. We pray. Then we allow God to answer those prayers however He sees fit." He pointed out that everything his church had done—its vision statement, its planning documents, the selection of staff and lay leaders, the decisions about new programs—were the result of prayers.

3. *These churches had learned to celebrate the fruits of prayer.* When a prayer had been answered in a miraculous way, or even in a way that reduced pressure or tension, the church was invited to offer additional prayers of thanks for the goodness of God in caring for His people. Prayer was made more acceptable to the people in these churches because they were used to hearing not only about the tragedies and anxieties which required prayer for help, but also of the wonderful, unimagined solutions to difficult situations. As one pastor described his approach to celebrating victory through prayer, "When you get a gift from God, He deserves a thank-you note. We look at prayers of thanksgiving as our means of acknowledging His work and expressing our gratitude."

4. *The congregation was held accountable for prayer.* While I did not encounter any church that had developed quantified

means of evaluating prayer (nor is such a means desirable), the leaders of the healthy churches consistently inquired about the prayer life of the church. It was common to hear the pastor or other leaders ask people about their "daily quiet time" or to push people to be sure they were in touch with what God was trying to tell them. A few churches recommended that people engage in written tracking of prayer—requests they made of God, answers they had received and questions raised through their prayer interaction that needed to be resolved through additional prayer and study.

MARKS OF A PRAYING CHURCH

The perceived value of prayer within a church is evident through the ways in which prayer is integrated into the corporate activities of the church. In the worship services of the targeted churches, the pastors prayed in a heartfelt manner. Theirs was not the prayer of a performer or an individual following the standard ritual expected of a minister. Of equal importance was the fact that although the worship services, in particular, demanded sensitivity to the timing of the elements of the service, prayer was never shortchanged. Several pastors indicated that they would rather reduce the time allotted to their sermons than to minimize or abbreviate the time in which the congregation was in conversation with God.

People in the congregation were allowed to pray as led, either silently or perhaps in short public prayers. The size of the church, in some cases, dictated the ways in which people's prayers were integrated into the Body life.

In classes—Sunday School, midweek, special series—prayer was a standard, but nonroutine part of the corporate experience. Different forms of prayer were used. In some instances, although prayer was not the subject matter of the class, the initial portion of the class time was devoted to a short lesson on prayer, with a follow-up experience of that lesson. Sometimes people were encouraged to break into small groups within the class and to participate in prayer in these more intimate clusters. There was generally a sensitivity to those people who were not comfortable with public prayer, enabling them to keep to themselves until they felt comfortable praying in front of others. In the same way, small groups that met during the week were encouraged to make prayer a vital element in the weekly meeting time.

In staff meetings, prayer was not simply a cursory period of time spent on an obligatory religious activity. It almost seemed that some of these churches felt defenseless without a significant portion of their time together committed to praying for and with each other. The time was used to truly seek the mind and heart of God in preparation for decisions, interaction and reflection.

More often than not, these churches had groups of people whose sole ministry was to pray for those who requested or needed prayer support. They had other teams whose primary ministry was to pray for the leaders of the church, and to pray during the services and classes that people would be met by God in powerful ways. They had well-attended retreats devoted to prayer and meditation, times during which people could leave the anxieties and pressures of careers and household responsibilities behind just long enough to listen to what God has to say to them. They had prayer teams whose dominant ministry was to provide healing—emotional, psychological, sometimes physical—to those in need.

In short, prayer was every bit as high-profile a ministry in these bodies as was preaching, counseling, youth ministry and missions. Again, this was part of the vision of the church: to be in tune with God's will for the church, as determined partially through the experience of prayer.

TAKING INVENTORY

If you were to track the prayer life of the staff members of your church, what would you uncover? Do they pray consistently, intensively, expectantly? Do they pray for the church with a sense of urgency? Are their prayers inwardly focused?

If you were to trace the prayer-related teaching and behavior your staff publicly models for your congregation, how would they rate? How often do they incorporate meaningful prayer into their behavior? You cannot expect to have a congregation that takes prayer seriously if the leaders of the church do not commit their lives to a relationship with God that is built upon a significant prayer life.

When was the last time your church celebrated answered prayer, other than in relation to a stewardship campaign? If people never witness exuberance over God's responses to our prayers, chances are good that they won't think of prayer as an exciting, productive endeavor.

When the people of your church make major decisions in their personal lives, do they pray for guidance in those decisions? What would it take to get your people to make prayer a consistent part of their daily decision-making?

How much do your people know about prayer? In some churches, prayer forms the foundation of the "equipping" that is provided for living a Christian life. Could your people identify the different purposes or types of prayer? Have they been shown the value and potential of prayer in tangible, real ways? It would be inexcusable for any body of believers not to be involved in prayer simply due to ignorance. Is prayer one of the spiritual disciplines taken for granted by your church?

In many stagnant churches, to have a "prayer ministry" means that you are either uninvolved in "real" Christianity or that you are not in the mainstream of the church's life. Too often, churches subconsciously develop a hierarchy of ministry talents; and prayer tends to be located at the bottom of the hierarchy. In your church, are men and women who are dedicated to prayer esteemed as significant contributors to the church's ministry? Is it viewed as an honor and a privilege to partake in the church's prayer ministry—or is it simply a way of placating

those deemed to be "spiritual leftovers," a gentle way of informing a person that he or she has no other tangible or valued gifts
to offer the Body?

In an age in which the stakes are growing ever higher in the
daily spiritual battles of all people, prayer is indisputably one of
the greatest—and most under-utilized—weapons we have at our
disposal. If this examination of the experience of growing
churches teaches us nothing else, we must grasp the importance
of a vibrant prayer ministry.

11 INVESTING IN TOMORROW'S LEADERS

IN EACH CHURCH EXAMINED FOR THIS BOOK, I FOUND THAT THE LEAD-
ers believed that ministering to young people was a key to having a growing, healthy church. Why? Here are some of the reasons they gave.

Ministering to kids is one way of attracting adults. In some
cases, the adults are looking for a means of ingraining the values of the church in their kids, but they need help doing so. In
other cases, parents are moved by the genuine compassion for
their kids exhibited by the church. Regardless, many adults feel
at home in a place that sincerely accepts their offspring.

Kids represent the highest potential for conversion. While
some of the churches were not aware of the actual statistics,
they intuitively and experientially realized that a comparative-
ly large proportion of the youngsters they encountered came
to accept Christ as their Savior. (Nationwide, our research suggests that two out of every three adults who are Christian made
the decision to accept Christ as Savior before they reached the
age of 18.) Thus, ministry to young people was viewed as a
means of efficient evangelism.[1]

*Kids have a way of impacting the church environment
dynamically.* They can breathe new life into a stale environ-

ment, or kill it altogether to allow for a new and livelier environment. As adults, we have a tendency to memorialize things in programs and routines, frequently removing the spontaneity and enthusiasm from the activity. Remaining sensitive to the interests and reactions of young people enabled these churches to maintain a sense of vitality and adventure that might otherwise have been trapped in "proper" organizational techniques.

Today's youth are the leaders of tomorrow. A church that does little to foster mature leaders will be a church void of capable leadership in the future. The healthy churches were proud to list the names of adults who had grown up through the church youth program, and were now either leaders in that church or had moved on to significant ministries in other areas of the country. The church had invested heavily in building a spiritual foundation in those young people, targeting them as a primary route to achieving spiritual reproduction. These congregations felt they had received a substantial return on that spiritual investment and felt that this, in itself, made the emphasis upon ministry to children and adolescents worthwhile.

Offspring frequently have a more profound effect on the spiritual development of their parents than do the pastor or church staff. Although there was no quantification of this phenomenon, many examples were cited of children playing an instrumental role in the spiritual renewal of their parents, either through direct testimony or through the impact on the parents of the change that had overtaken their child as a result of their church experience.

Kids serve as a creative testing ground for new ministry ideas. On occasion, untried concepts for programs or communications would be tested with the young people. The greatest value of such tests was not the ability to project the success of a new ministry venture based on the youths' reactions. Rather, it was the assurance that kids would provide honest feedback, enabling the church leaders to sharpen or forget about the program or communication.

Undeniably, working with kids these days is a fascinating experience. The leaders at the growing churches concurred that ministering to children and youth today is even more demanding than in the past. Raised in a society in which cut-throat competition is commonplace, they are exposed to excellence in the quality of products and services, and they have come to expect excellence from the church, too. Today's young people are quality driven. They are not willing to accept mediocrity or to put up with ministry that is in a maintenance mode.

ADDRESSING THE NEEDS OF CHILDREN AND YOUTH

We may have unsurpassed opportunities for influencing the lives of young people, but we also have unprecedented demands in terms of the nature of the outreach we provide. Given this realization, the leaders of the healthy churches acknowledged that for their ministry to be complete, it must identify and address the needs of children and youth. They were just as quick to note that this is no small order. Remaining relevant among kids is perhaps more elusive than among adults.

Further, impacting the youth market means understanding the needs and hot buttons of different age groups and subcultures within age groups. For instance, ministries that meet the needs of preschoolers are very different from what cuts to the heart of today's teenager. And within the teen segment, there are very specialized segments—kids from blended families, kids with low self-esteem, those from poor families, overachievers, etc.— all of which require personalized ministry.

The leaders of the growing churches generally believed that the ways in which kids respond to different teaching tech niques and materials change more rapidly than is true among adults. Although it was taxing to stay current and relevant among youth, these leaders unanimously deemed those efforts worthwhile.

Approaches to Ministry

Perhaps surprisingly, no one children's or youth ministry strategy was common to all of the growing churches. Despite compatible perspectives about ministry to them, each church had its own way of dealing with kids.

There were, however, a few common approaches. Kids attending church programs (Sunday School or midweek groups) were divided by age group or grade level. Many of these churches had thrown out the standardized Sunday School and midweek curriculum and fashioned their own approach to educating. (Some used standardized curriculum, but substantially tailored it to their own special needs and approach.)

Exercises in Organized Chaos

A common characteristic among the youth programs of successful churches was that they encouraged creativity on the part of teachers/leaders—and they expected the programs to be exercises in organized chaos. They acknowledged that these were kids, not adults, and that it was important to permit them to have ample time to behave like kids.

A number of the church leaders I spoke with decried the fact that America seems committed to robbing kids of their childhood, forcing them to accept responsibility and engage in adult-oriented activities before they were mature. At their church, they had decided, it would be permissible for a kid to act out childhood behavior (within boundaries) and to explore his or her world and self within the guidance offered through a loosely structured, but values-driven, youth program.

Games and Activities

More often than not, the youth programs featured games and competitive activities. A common approach, especially in the programs for adolescents, was the Son City form of ministry, in which kids are divided into teams and compete for points

Raised in a society with cut-throat competition, today's youth have come to expect excellence from church. They are quality driven, unwilling to accept mediocrity.

during the initial portion of the group meeting. In such competition, winning was acknowledged as being important—but not as important as building a cohesive team, and being supportive of each other's efforts.

Communication was a key goal in these exercises. The games themselves were merely vehicles for promoting the types of skills that the church believed to be important ingredients in the make-up of a functional human being and church activist.

Adolescents

When it came to teaching, the ministry to adolescents placed a greater emphasis upon the individual's response to social issues and upon facilitating relationships than is found in most churches. This was a conscious outgrowth of the church's philosophy that a vital part of its function is service, and that service requires us to be in personal relationship with other people.

Regardless of the age of the kids involved, though, the activities and teaching tended to be contemporary and upbeat. Teachers/leaders were coached by the youth department staff to avoid boring, bookish lessons that communicated the notion that church is no fun. "I'm working with the MTV generation here," one youth director explained. "If we harp on one activity for more than 10 minutes at a time, we lose their attention. Like it? Of course I don't like it. But that's what we have to work with, so we have to be creative within the boundaries of how these kids approach life."

Most of these churches went out of their way to incorporate technology whenever feasible. Using videotapes (some self-produced, others prerecorded and available in the marketplace), contemporary music and computer-designed graphics to communicate ideas, the leaders were constantly on the lookout for ways to communicate that made their material easy to understand and yet culturally relevant to the age group being addressed.

A Wide Array of Leaders

These churches even had a different slant on who should be youth leaders. They were intent upon involving as many adults from the church body as possible, not just the parents of young people. By incorporating the energy and creativity of young adults with the wisdom and experience of older adults, the activities and insights related to the youth and ministry were broadened. Even more critical for the overall outreach and development of the church at large, involving such a wide range of adults helped the congregation to feel ownership of the church's youth ministry and to capture a sense of excitement and hope for the future.

Another key distinctive of growing churches was that the youth pastor was not viewed as simply a junior staff person. In many churches, the youth minister is thought of as the person seeking to get the experience that will enable him to move up the hierarchy of responsibility within the church. Across the board, youth ministers tend to be underpaid, because of the low value of their work in the eyes of the church. Consequently, youth pastors often look upon the job as a stepping stone to "real ministry."

In successful churches, however, the youth pastors were people who had no ambition of "rising" beyond youth pastor, or any intention of "graduating" to adult ministry. They invariably talked about a "calling" to work with kids, and the fulfillment they received from the post. When asked what they aspired to in the long run, their dreams related to expanding the ministry to young people at their current church, or to serving in even more influential and aggressive youth ministries at other churches. They viewed ministry to kids as a productive, satisfying and esteemed endeavor. They looked forward to moving up in youth ministry, rather than moving outside of it.

TAKING INVENTORY

Does your church have a youth and children's program, or a baby-sitting service? It became very clear that ministries to young people in the growing churches showed respect for who young people are, and an understanding of the myriad of pressures they live with. To be embraced as a relevant part of the lives of the kids being touched, the program had to be more than a place where they were deposited by parents for safe-keeping during the adult time of worship or learning.

If your church has a youth program, what would make it attract the kinds of kids who wind up in street gangs, or who spend their free time selling drugs to other kids? More than ever, churches are finding that to attract kids they must offer practical alternatives to the options kids have before them. That means providing a positive environment, a relaxed atmosphere and information that is relevant to their daily struggles. This principle was every bit as critical to reaching eight-year-old children as those who were 18.

Do you see your youth as evangelistic agents? The evidence suggests that they can be effective at getting their parents to take God, Jesus Christ and the Christian life more seriously. (A few of the pastors indicated that the track record shows that kids were actually *more* effective in evangelism than were the adult-oriented ministries offered by the church.) Do your programs prepare kids to interact with their parents about spiritual matters?

What is the status of your youth pastor? Does he receive a salary, benefits, program resources, staff status and support that is equivalent to that given to other staff persons? Examine the role of the youth pastor, from expectations to rewards. If your youth director is not capable of leading a strong youth program, make the appropriate changes in how that very special ministry is being led. And once you have a person with the vision and energy to make a youth ministry work, it is in the church's best interest for it to take care of that critically important staff person.

What is the congregation's image of the children's and youth ministry? Do they understand the importance of an effective youth outreach? Are they kept well-informed of what is happening through that vital outreach? Are they willing to personally become supportive, through time, money, prayer or other means? Remember, the congregation generally takes its cues from the senior pastor. If he has not put his full weight behind the youth ministry, it is imperative that such support be given. Anything less will handicap a ministry to young people right from the start.

Note
1. George Barna, *The Church Today: Insightful Statistics and Commentary* (Glendale, CA: Barna Research Group, 1990).

SECTION III

STRUCTURE AND LEADERSHIP

What then shall we say, brothers? When you come together, everyone has a hymn, or a word of instruction, a revelation, a tongue or an interpretation. All of these must be done for the strengthening of the church....For God is not a God of disorder but of peace. . . . Everything should be done in a fitting and orderly way (1 Cor. 14:26, 33, 40).

THUS FAR, WE HAVE EXAMINED THE COMMONALITIES RELATED TO how growing, user friendly churches approach ministry, and what they do to impact the lives of people. But what about the ways they organize and direct the church so their perspectives and activities related to ministry can flourish?

Each of the successful churches we examined had in common several characteristics related to leadership and organizational structure—to doing things "in a fitting and orderly way" (1 Cor. 14:40). While having these factors in place would, in themselves, not be enough to catapult a church into a growth mode, they do appear to be important foundations that enable growth to emerge.

These factors are partially a result of systems that have been developed to help organize and manage the ministry, and partially a result of having a pragmatic philosophy of management that serves the ends of the church.

In all cases, it became apparent that the systems and structures, just like the ministry programs described earlier, were perceived to be valuable and worthy of keeping *only as long as they served the people who were making the church's ministry happen.* In other words, if a system or structure proved to be an obstacle to growth or ministry, the system came under review. If necessary, it was altered, replaced or removed. Invariably, the bottom line was ministry impact. The churches that were making a difference in people's lives believed that systems and structures were defensible only if they facilitated outreach and moved the church closer to achieving its goals.

In comparing these growing churches with those that are less successful, it seemed that denominational churches and churches based upon tradition and ritual had the greatest difficulty developing systems and structures that serve the people. Their tendency was to have people acquiesce to systems and structures. In the tradition-based churches, especially, there seemed to be a greater premium put upon the perpetuation of the systems and structures than upon the quality of the ministry.

While allegiance to denominational practices and time-honored traditions can play an important part in ministry, if growth is a goal of the church there is likely to be tension between the historical and the newly-created approaches to ministry. In some instances, it was that very tension that helped to clarify a church's ultimate priorities.

In this section we will note four common factors related to organization structure and leadership among the successful, growing churches studied for this report. ➡

12 UNYIELDING FLEXIBILITY

No SINGLE ORGANIZATIONAL STRUCTURE OR FORMAT WAS COMMON to all of the user friendly churches. In comparing the ways these churches allocated authority and put structure to ministry activity, variety was evident. Organizational charts differed from church to church. Job titles and key roles varied from congregation to congregation. Even the numbers of decision-making units varied considerably across the sample of churches.

This lack of conformity was not surprising. Although the successful churches did not utilize a common structure, they did subscribe to a common philosophy: *the ministry is not called to fit the church's structure; the structure exists to further effective ministry.*

A COMMITMENT TO MINISTRY OVER STRUCTURE

These churches had a keen sense of direction and purpose (i e , vision and plans). Their top priority was to achieve their ministry goals. If the organizational charts and structural procedures inhibited such ministry, they would cautiously but willingly work around the barriers. They were not about to let a man-made system hinder their ability to take advantage of a God-given opportunity to change lives for the Kingdom.

Structure, in fact, was not an issue in these churches. Certainly, these congregations were led by individuals who see the wisdom of developing and maintaining orderly processes. They recognized the importance of a formal hierarchy of authority, and the importance of avoiding anarchy (even if the intentions of the anarchists are good). But structure was viewed as a support system, a means to an end, rather than an end in itself. The structures they used had been developed, accepted, implemented, reevaluated and upgraded. At all times, the focus was upon ministry not structure.

Overcoming Structural Conflicts

The leaders of these churches occasionally conceived or approved programs and policies which conflicted with existing systems and structures. Such decisions typically raised only a brief discussion about the inconsistency between an outreach and a structure. Little time was devoted to agonizing over how to alter a program so that it coincided with prevailing systems and structures. The church leaders were far more likely to ignore inconsistencies or merely note them, as long as they were confident that the likely ministry outcome justified the conflict with the structure. In some of the growing churches studied, the leaders were more likely to change the structure than to limit a ministry opportunity.

It follows, then, that these churches were generally *able to respond quickly and decisively to a situation*. They may have had committees and commissions within their structure, but they tended not to be weighed down by having to wait for decisions from a body that convened only occasionally. In some instances, such groups retained the responsibility for decision-making, but created mechanisms which facilitated rapid response to unforeseen situations.

For instance, some churches had committees that made key

Holding fast to outdated systems or structures that look feasible on paper, but in fact strangle the life out of the organism, is self-defeating.

decisions on the basis of a series of telephone conversations with committee members, rather than waiting for the opportunity to establish a face-to-face meeting. In other instances, the group delegated its decision-making authority under specified conditions to a designated leader from within the group, who was accountable to the group.

Finding a Balance

Thus, although the organizational structure may not have carried substantial weight within the church, and the ability to easily change that structure was generally a distinguishing characteristic of these churches, the buck *did* stop somewhere. And everyone knew *where* the buck stopped. Decision-making was not so decentralized that there was not a single individual to whom the church would turn for a final determination on a thorny issue. In the same vein, the church knew where to turn when a program had gone sour, and someone had to be held accountable for bad decisions or insufficient monitoring of performance. In most cases, that person was the pastor or the pastor's designated leader.

In most cases, the senior pastor was not really an organizational stickler. Generally, his concern was with results more than process. He often relied upon someone on staff (e.g., the business administrator) to keep track of organizational issues, freeing him to concentrate on people and ministry.

Is this approach healthy? In today's fast-changing world, efficient ministry is characterized by the ability to adapt quickly to newly recognized needs. Holding fast to outdated systems or structures that look feasible on paper, but in fact strangle the life out of the organism, is self-defeating. The balance that must be achieved is one between flexibility and spinelessness.

Some churches, in their desire to be sensitive to their environment, have gone overboard in their flexibility. They emerge as almost structureless, paralyzed by their lack of backbone in the process. Frequently, such churches also lack the clear sense of purpose and plans that enabled the growing churches studied for this book to know when and where to draw the lines.

TAKING INVENTORY

How much time does your leadership team or staff spend discussing structural limitations or configurations? If your meetings and attempts to move ahead with ministry are hindered by protracted discussions about structure, the structure itself may need an overhaul. Similarly, if the discussions end with the determination that a specific form of ministry with a high potential for success cannot be conducted because "that's not the way that we do things," you may be suffering from an improper structure.

When decisions are made, is there an ultimate decision maker, a single individual who has the final right of approval or disapproval? If not, your church may suffer from a structure that has decentralized power too greatly, essentially rendering the Body leaderless. Just as an organization can be smothered by a leader or group that wields too much power, so can a church wither if it fails to have one individual or *small* group of people who are responsible and held accountable for all ministry decisions.

One of the great debilitators of churches is the requirement that committees make ministry decisions. The reality is that committees are best at meeting, not making decisions. Unless the committee is small in number, focused in purpose and manned by capable individuals, the likelihood of valuable decisions or leadership emerging from that group is minimal.

Suppose your church had an opportunity to implement a ministry that had a high potential for positive impact, but needed to get started immediately. Could your church spring into action within hours or, at the most, a few days? If not, consider the possibility that your church is weighed down either by ineffective leaders, or by a structure that is too cumbersome to exploit meaningful opportunities provided by God.

Are key leaders in your church becoming frustrated by their inability to work through the system to get things done? Sometimes, this is an indication not of a bad structure, but of a person who is in the wrong position. Before you scrap an aspect of your organizational plan, study the qualities of the people who are having difficulty navigating through that system. It may be that the structure is satisfactory, but the positions assigned to individuals within the structure need reconsideration.

Is your structure something that you are willing to reexamine? That is, would you and your leaders be willing to overhaul the entire structure and all the systems now in place if you were reasonably sure that your overall ministry could be enhanced? If you are not willing to take such a bold step, you might reconsider your motivations for ministry, and your understanding of God's call upon your life.

Nowhere in Scripture did Jesus get tangled up in organizational theory. His was a ministry of efficiency and simplicity. It worked for Him. Although our society is much more complex, and the decisions we are called to make may be more involved, chances are that simplicity is still the best solution.

13 THERE'S NO SUBSTITUTE FOR A REAL LEADER

User friendly churches invariably had a strong pastor leading the church. "Strong" means that the pastor was in control and was a true leader. "Pastor" refers to one who understood the needs of the congregation and the target audience and provided the necessary vision and spiritual guidance. A strong pastor is one who takes charge of the church without breaking the spirit of those who wish to be involved.

PORTRAIT OF AN EFFECTIVE PASTOR

A strong pastor is one who has a firm grasp of the big picture. He has a clear sense of God's vision for the church, and an understanding of his personal calling within that framework. This person is in tune with the details of what is going on in the church, but is not bogged down by them. He understands how important it is for someone at the church to address all of the day-to-day activities and minute decisions that must occur for effective ministry to happen. However, *he* is not likely to be the person who will plunge into all of the details of every program and activity undertaken by the church.

Consider the contrasting leadership styles of Jimmy Carter

and Ronald Reagan. Carter entered the White House with a sociopolitical agenda and sought to enforce that vision for the nation. Unfortunately, his leadership style was such that he was involved in all levels of decision-making and became overwhelmed in the operational minutiae of the government. Consequently, his administration was able to effect relatively limited change during his one term in office.

Reagan, on the other hand, left the details of state to his lieutenants. He focused on the larger goals and strategies associated with his agenda. The tactical operations were turned over to his associates. He saw his job as focusing on the big picture, and making sure that capable people were on top of the details that were important in the move toward making the big picture come to fruition.

Both men had their successes and failures in office. But history will show that more policy and programmatic changes were accomplished during the Reagan administration, largely because he was willing to have specialists address details, freeing him for more pressing concerns.

The Gift of Delegation

In much the same way, I found that the leaders of the growing churches delegated responsibility without anxiety. It seemed that those pastors perceived delegation as a means to an end: it was a way to empower other people to do ministry. At the same time, it provided the senior pastor the freedom to concentrate on the areas of giftedness which probably allowed him to rise to the position of senior pastor in the first place. In my estimation, few of these men were truly gifted administrators. Their gifts were in the areas of teaching, communications and leadership. For them to have become bogged down in other aspects of the ministry would have been to abuse their gifts and stifle the church.

In contrast, pastors of stagnant churches often reject the impulse to delegate, largely because they fear it may diminish their own significance in the church, or that the people to whom the responsibility is delegated might fail. In either case, the result is stunted ministry, in which the pastor continues to bear the brunt of responsibility for ministry. Often, he crumbles under the weight of that responsibility.

The Gift of Confidence

Pastors of the user friendly congregations had enough confidence in themselves as leaders that they believed the only way they could flourish was by getting others to take on responsibility. They saw the power of a larger work force, even if one possible tradeoff was diminished quality or productivity. Knowing that, as senior pastor, they retained the ultimate responsibility for all that is done within the church, motivated them to consciously direct their efforts toward enhancing the output of those who ministered on behalf of the church. That is, the pastor truly became a leader of people rather than a line worker.

The Gift of Interaction

One of the struggles for the pastors was to be a partner in ministry with the people. Image is a critical part of the leadership process. To convey the appearance of being above the battle fray would undermine a pastor's rapport with the congregation, their trust in his leadership and his impact as a model for other church leaders. While he could not afford to spend all of his time addressing minor issues or taking part in every meeting and outreach activity, he did have to have a consistent presence and relationship with both his staff and church members.

Most of the pastors involved in this study handled this challenge by having frequent, meaningful interaction with the leaders of the various outreach activities and programs sponsored by the church. They would also acknowledge current activity publicly, helping the people of the church to feel that the ministry in which they were engaged was important, and part of the master plan for ministry of the church. These pastors also had personal ministries that were known to the congregation. This seemed to inspire people to take their own ministries more seriously.

The Gift of Decision-making

Although they knew how to delegate authority, these pastors were not afraid to make a decision. In fact, they seemed to enjoy it. They liked to see action spring forth as a result of their decisiveness. They had an entrepreneurial spirit that enabled them to envision possibilities, conceive ways of making those possibilities come to fruition, and marshal and direct the resources to make good things happen. Frequently they created opportunities to make the gospel relevant and practical. They tended to be proactive more than reactive. While this tendency is unusual among pastors, it seemed possible as a result of their refusal to get bogged down by the details. By keeping the vision in mind, and having a working awareness of the day-to-day activities of the church, they were able to be more visionary than functionary.

The Gift of Visibility

One attribute of the strong pastor was that he was visible. While he did not seek the spotlight, he tended to be in the right place at the right time. Again, it appeared that this ability to remain *in* focus without being *the* focus of the church was because he had a sense of the big picture, and thus was more apt to know where the "right place" was at any given moment. He had his finger on the pulse of the ministry, and could determine where his presence would be most effective.

Often a strong pastor would be present at a special activity, even if he was not integrally involved with that particular aspect of ministry. He desired to be present because he recognized that his presence lent an aura of credibility and significance to the ministry, and that it told people that he was in touch with what

Leaders of the growing churches delegated responsibility without anxiety. They perceived delegation as a means to an end: it was a way to empower other people to do ministry.

was truly happening in the church. He took delight in lending his valuable time and presence to support the ministries delegated to and carried out by others.

The strong pastor felt no guilt at having merely a symbolic role in the development and success of various facets of the church's ministry. With only a limited number of hours each day in which to accomplish the many tasks on his agenda, the strong pastor knew—and sometimes learned from harsh experience—that it is better to have something to show for the day, accomplished mostly through the efforts of others, than to have great ideas that never made it off the drawing board, or that suffered due to lack of attention. It would be preferable to be a symbolic part of a success than an integral part of a failure.

The Gift of Practicality

A minister who operates strictly as a teacher/preacher, and does little else to move the church forward, is not a strong pastor. Teaching and preaching are indeed valuable gifts. Good teaching and preaching are characteristic of an effective church. However, a real *leader* is not simply one who speaks about ministry, then walks away from the battle front to study for the next lesson to be taught. The strong pastor is a *model* for people. He may be scholarly, but his teaching is not strictly academic. He is a leader, but his leadership is practical, not theoretical.

The Gift of Accountability

The strong pastor also recognizes and accepts ultimate accountability for the nature and quality of all ministry being done by that church. To be a leader means accepting that responsibility. Because of the serious nature of this responsibility, the strong pastor is cautious about the delegation of authority, but not paralyzed by the fear of bad decisions. It is the element of risk, perhaps, that makes this aspect of the pastorate exciting and interesting to these people.

The pastors of the successful churches studied were the first to admit that they do make some bad decisions. However, they were also quick to note that they do not make the same bad decision twice. They learn from their mistakes—quickly and efficiently. Because they understood their unique role in the life of the church, they accepted responsibility for their errors, moved swiftly to rectify (not cover up) their bad decisions and cataloged that experience for future reference. Since the pastors were on top of what was happening in all phases of the church, these churches rarely experienced problems that festered over long periods of time. Analysis and response happened consistently and quickly in these churches.

The Gift of Discernment

Perhaps one distinction between pastors of growing churches and those of stagnant congregations has to do with the ability to recognize a bad decision. In some of the stagnant churches I studied, there were some decisions which seemed responsible for the lifeless state of the church. Yet, not only was the pastor prepared to commit the same error; that error was not recognized as a mistake. The gift of discernment may be one of the more valuable gifts provided to the pastors of leading churches.

TAKING INVENTORY

If the pastor of the church is more interested in being *recognized* as the leader of a growing church than in *being* the leader of a growing church, that person may not be the right pastor for your congregation. If the individual is turned on by the spotlight, chances are better than average that he is not the type of leader who can lead a church into *sustained* growth. There may be a spurt of growth, but maintaining the energy, excitement and impact of the initial burst is unlikely. In other words, there may not be a sufficient depth of ministry to enable the church to continue to meet people's needs after the exhilaration of sudden or rapid success wears off.

Is your church led by a pastor who is so hands-on that nothing gets done unless he has seen detailed plans, discussed every aspect of those plans with the people involved and participated in the implementation of those plans? If so, you have an administrator or a policy-maker, but not a true leader. The church is likely to suffer because that pastor will slow down the process and smother the life from many of the programs. Would it make sense to redefine the role of that person, shifting the actual leadership responsibilities to someone who is more inclined to possess a strategic vision and to make things happen than he is to study them?

How often does the pastor support ministries emanating from the church? Only when it is related to an issue that tugs at his heart strings? Stand back for a moment and try to determine if that selective support approach has prevented some worthy ministries from taking off or from reaching their potential. If so, reconsider whether or not the pastor is using the power of his position in the most effective way possible.

By nature, strong pastors are agreeable but confrontational. They do not aggressively look for fights, nor do they take pleasure in going head-to-head with a person or group. However, the churches that get ahead are led by pastors who are willing to confront individuals or groups when such a confrontation is called for. They pick their battles wisely, but stand their ground once the battles have been picked. Is your church led by a pastor who carefully picks battles, or by one who constantly seeks to create compromise between differing viewpoints? In none of the healthy churches examined was the leader wishy-washy. They believed that for a church to get ahead, some tough stands must be taken. And they were willing to face the heat such stands generated. Does your church have such a leader?

If the people of your church were asked to identify the personal ministry of the pastor, other than his pulpit ministry, could they accurately identify something? Today, both believers and nonbelievers are constantly watching Christian leaders, anxious to put Christianity to the test and see if it is real. In local churches, people are skeptical of pastors who talk about ministry, but are not actively engaged in ministry beyond the pulpit. Part of being a strong pastor is being an active minister. While the people may not share the same interest or passion as the pastor for his particular ministry focus, they ought to at least know that he is involved in forms of ministry other than preaching and administration.

14 WHOSE CHURCH IS IT, ANYWAY?

IN SUCCESSFUL CHURCHES, WHILE THE PASTOR WAS USUALLY A DOMI-nant leader, he was ultimately a *team player*. It was the team orientation that enabled these churches to disperse authority and responsibility, and move forward.

The situation in these churches was similar to the time in Israel's history when Moses was called to be their leader. No figure in biblical times was a stronger individualist than Moses. This is the man who was authoritative enough that he could make his people drink water laced with gold dust in punish-ment for making and worshiping the golden calf (see Exod. 32:15-20). Yet Moses was not threatened by shared leadership. He was able to take the advice of his father-in-law Jethro, and delegate part of the responsibility for ruling the people to deputies, leaving much of the day-to-day responsibility to them (see Exod. 18). He did not need to inject his presence in every decision.

THE PASTOR AS TEAM LEADER

The growing churches we studied had pastors who, as Moses, were not afraid to accept final responsibility for the flock. This role meant that they stood in the spotlight on a regular basis. But, again following the pattern of Moses, they were not afraid to share the spotlight and to delegate leadership responsibilities or to be absent from some decision-making situations. The pastor's position as a focus of attention was but one of many focal points the church had to offer. In the end, the outreach of the church may have had the pastor as front man, but his influence was only as strong as the support team backing him. In successful churches, those teams were deep both in numbers and in capabilities.

Periods of Absence

A strategy that worked well for most growing churches was to have the pastor away from the church for a *planned absence*. Those periods of absence were generally planned a year or so in advance, and were purposeful: e.g., for study leave, participation in a sister ministry, or some other reason that was valued in the eyes of the congregation and the pastor.

Interestingly, when these pastors had such a planned escape, they did not always use the time for study or for relaxation. Occasionally, they would seek out opportunities for new forms of ministry in which they could sharpen their skills. In some cases, this meant going overseas and laboring as a temporary missionary. In other instances, it meant serving as a guest teacher at a college or seminary. A few pastors took the time to visit other churches, observing different ministries in action, and learning more about what was and was not working for other churches.

Ministry as Avocation

Such behavior points to a common attribute of these leaders: while the job of leading a church was exhausting, *they loved being involved in ministry*. Ministry, to these men, was nearly as much an avocation as a vocation.

How often have you watched someone in the entertainment

In the growing churches, the brief absence of the senior pastor actually strengthened the church by making the rest of the team work together as a unit. They experienced the joy of knowing that the church was not a one-man show.

field, whether it is sports, music, or theater, and asked yourself how fair it is that they get paid for their efforts? To these church leaders, ministry was in the same category: enjoyable and fulfilling, yet it provided them with a decent living. Many people use vacation time as an escape from their normal activities. To the leaders of these churches, having a time to escape the daily pressure was a much needed breather, but that did not necessarily mean that they would isolate themselves from interaction with ministry even during their break periods.

As much as the pastors gained from their leave, though, it is likely that the greatest benefit was realized by their congregations. During the pastor's absence, the staff and laity realized that *they* were the church, and were quite capable of furthering the ministry without the pastor. Certainly, his presence was a key ingredient in the overall ministry mix. Given a choice, they would unquestionably choose to have the senior pastor in the lead role, using his gifts to orchestrate the entire ministry.

More Than a One-man Show

In the growing churches I studied, the brief absence of the senior pastor actually *strengthened* the church by making the rest of the team work together as a unit. It enabled them to experience the joy of knowing that the church was not a one-man show, a collection of capable individuals whose abilities were smothered by the leader. Instead, such an absence provided them with the opportunity to make progress without wondering if the church was simply a ministry of the pastor. And they generally sought to make progress, rather than remain in a state of suspended ministry, until the return of the head honcho.

If my experiences and observations are accurate, it seems clear that a healthy church is one which is not exclusively dependent upon the pastor for the final decisions on all programs and events. The pastor is ideally more of a defender of the vision and dispenser of authority and encouragement than an operations manager. In the churches involved in this study, pastors became a CEO (chief executive officer) as the church grew and matured, not a COO (chief operating officer).

This means, however, that when the pastor is gone from the scene, he must be willing to let his colleagues who are left in charge make decisions. In stagnant churches, the pastor often requires that any significant decisions regarding the church be submitted for his approval. If he is on vacation, therefore, he will leave his telephone number to be reached in case of an emergency. If the absence is a brief one, all meaningful decisions are to be held in abeyance, until his return. Because that pastor cannot let go of the reigns of ministry, his flock becomes paralyzed. They lose the ability to make good decisions and to carry them through without someone constantly looking over their shoulder.

In the growing churches, the pastor demonstrated sufficient trust and confidence in his people to allow them to make important decisions without his input. He was willing to live with the consequences of those decisions. These men generally believed that they had done a satisfactory job in communicating the vision of the ministry and the direction of the church. One way of finding out—and thereafter releasing the pressure they felt regarding decision-making—was to entrust his ministry partners with decision-making authority, and see how well they could do.

A Link in the Chain

A few of the pastors of growing churches confided that it was not easy for them to get used to the idea that they were not the irreplaceable link in the chain of ministry. "Quite honestly, I was crushed," laughed one senior pastor, leader of a large charismatic congregation. "I returned and found that things were going more smoothly than when I left. At first I felt unnecessary, like I was an extra piece of furniture. But then I recognized that *this was the payoff*. For several years I had been working so hard to make these people self-supporting. Now, when it happened, it surprised the daylights out of me! But it has also become probably the most stress-relieving, satisfying compliment I could receive in response to what I've been trying to accomplish."

Time Away from Home

The pressures on the senior pastor at growing churches can be enormous. Time away from the daily grind of the church is absolutely necessary to restore and refresh the pastor. A church that is not willing to provide such time off will eventually burn out the pastor, and possibly extinguish the very flame of excitement and enthusiasm that ignited the church's growth.

All of the growing churches seemed to recognize the importance of allowing the pastor to get away and recharge his batteries in whatever manner he deemed most profitable. It is important to underscore the fact that the manner in which the break was spent was left up to the pastor. The lay leaders of the church did not attempt to identify for their pastor what was and what was not an "acceptable" absence.

My study uncovered a number of stagnant churches whose senior pastor was unwilling to leave for more than a week at a time each year. In some cases, this was due to the absence of other leaders capable of keeping the church moving forward for even the shortest of periods without the hand of the pastor in every decision. In other cases, the refusal to take time off was due to the insecurity of the pastor, who believed that if things went well in his absence, the congregation might deem him to be replaceable.

In either case, the final outcome was a pastor who constantly operated at less than full capacity, and a church that was not challenged to create the kinds of leaders and practices which would enhance a broad-based, healthy ministry —one that was more than just one man's vision, or the consequence of his capabilities.

One caution should be raised. A pair of pastors from growing churches became so brazen about the abilities of their church to function well in their absence that they began to abuse the privilege. One said, "I was much more open to accepting some of the numerous requests to speak at conferences, to visit other nations and to get involved in a wide range of exciting opportunities." He eventually discovered, however, that while his partners were quite capable of leading the church in his absence, a family that loses a member for extended periods of time begins to wonder how important they are to that individual.

"I began to lose touch with my people," the pastor said. "My relationships deteriorated, and I no longer really had my finger on the pulse of the church. When I was in town long enough to preach a few sermons, it felt a bit awkward because people never really knew who was in charge, or where I was in relation to the congregation. There wasn't enough continuity for them to grab on to. No amount of notoriety I gain while on the road, preaching at famous churches or giving keynotes at prestigious conferences, would deal with the needs of my congregation."

Continuity is an important consideration in the long-term health of the church. The occasional, planned absence of the pastor can allow the church to show what it is capable of doing thanks to the leadership provided by the pastor. But the extended absence of that leader can erode the spirit and enthusiasm of the church.

TAKING INVENTORY

What happens when the pastor at your church takes a vacation or study leave? Is there political maneuvering from within to realign systems and power? Is there confusion over what to do? Are people disinterested in attending services and meetings while he is away? Does the impact of the church wane in his absence? If so, reflect on whether your entire church is involved in ministry, or whether it is merely supporting one man who has a dynamic personal ministry.

It may prove useful to determine whether the church has taken the time and care to develop a sufficiently strong and deep leadership base to enable the Body to withstand the absence of the pastor. Ministries that have a true impact on the community are those that are more than a reflection of the interests and activities of the senior pastor. While the pastor is gone, does effective ministry continue to happen? Or is the church in a maintenance mode—a holding pattern while awaiting the return of the chief minister?

In some stagnant or declining churches, people seem to resent the time awarded to the pastor for vacation, study and renewal. This is indicative of churches that are inwardly focused, and dissatisfied with the quality and depth of the church's overall ministry. It is valuable to gain a sense of people's emotional reaction to the amount of time taken by the pastor for purposes such as vacation, renewal and study. If resentment is evident, it may suggest deeper concerns or problems related to people's perceptions of the leadership or ministry of the congregation.

By the same token, how much time does the pastor spend away from the church? A congregation that is healthy and growing is a congregation based upon relationships. A vital relationship is that between the pastor and his people. Absence may make the heart grow fonder, but too much absence may make the heart wander. Is the senior pastor sufficiently attentive to his own flock, or has his attention strayed too far afield?

15 INVESTING IN THE VOLUNTEER BANK

A CONGREGATION WE'LL CALL PRINCETON BAPTIST CHURCH WAS A small group, with fewer than 100 members. But like most churches, it believed in having a person assigned to each position on the organizational chart. One of those posts was Sunday School superintendent.

One morning in March the pastor received a call from the woman who was the current superintendent, indicating that she was resigning from the position—effective immediately. Panicking, the pastor raced through in his mind all of the potential replacements. It was a short list. He called his wife, discussed the possibilities with her and finally settled on Ken—one of the few people the pastor felt would accept the job.

Ken was a farmer by trade. He had not finished high school. He was a relatively new Christian, having accepted the Lord just a year earlier. But he had been faithful in attending both church and Sunday School, and he was well-liked by the other members.

When the pastor asked Ken to assume the prestigious post of Sunday School superintendent, Ken at first declined. He had never held a leadership position in a church, and wasn't sure what the job required. He had minimal formal education, and even less religious education. He told the pastor that he would feel uncomfortable in the position, although he would serve in any way the pastor felt was best for the church.

Eventually the pastor was able to talk Ken into taking on the duties of superintendent. After all, few others in the congregation would have the time or the willingness. And Ken would do his best at the job.

Sadly, Ken did not fare well as superintendent. He tried his best, but organizing teachers, lesson materials and educational programs was simply not his strength. He gave up after only a few months. His attendance at church and Sunday School became erratic. He was dropping out of church life because he felt he had let the church down, and that the experience had simply emphasized his personal shortcomings as an individual. It was a bad experience for all involved—even if it had plugged a hole in the church's organizational chart for a few months.

WHAT'S IN A VOLUNTEER

Unlike most organizations, churches rely heavily on a unique source of labor: volunteers. And unlike most churches, the user friendly ones in this study seemed to have an ample supply of qualified and capable people who were willing to surrender their most precious resources—time and ability—for the benefit of the church. Even more crucial was a conscious attempt to call out God's gifts in people, avoiding incidents such as Ken and his pastor experienced.

The key to establishing this available pool of laborers was the church's ability to help people realize the practical meaning of the New Testament teaching about servanthood, and the responsibilities we have as followers of Christ. These churches took great pains to lead people to understand that ministry is a give and take proposition.

To be a servant of Christ means getting in the trenches of ministry and doing what needs to be done to further God's kingdom—using the gifts He has given us. To be part of the church means accepting the responsibility to be a minister on behalf of the church. It also means that the church, usually through discerning leaders, has the responsibility not only to articulate the servant principle but to point out and affirm individual gifts.

What's Your Gift?

One of the actions that most clearly separated growing churches from stagnant churches, was the willingness of the growing bodies to accept people for who they were. Rather than take persons who volunteered their services and plug them into the most gaping hole that exists at the moment, user friendly churches first helped people to determine what God had called them to do. They believed that each person had an area of giftedness, and they strove to use that person's talents and skills in those areas. The responsibility of the church was to:

1. identify those gifts and talents;
2. refine those gifts;
3. provide opportunities for the individual to utilize those gifts in significant ministry; and
4. support the individual in that ministry.

By employing volunteers in the areas in which they are gifted, the probability of burnout, disenchantment with the church, disappointment with either the role they are asked to play or with the outcome of their own performance, is minimized. What tended to happen was that those involved in the ministry in areas of their own giftedness actually enjoyed what they did, and gained a sense of fulfillment from their involvement. Consequently, they were much happier about their church and their relationship with it. They looked forward to taking advantage of opportunities to minister because they were good at it. The prospect of the church impacting the community was substantially enhanced by making sure that people were not being asked to minister in ways which ignored their special strengths.

The Valued Volunteer

At successful churches, lay people were treated like professionals. This not only indicated the importance attached to the tasks being done by the individuals, but it also confirmed the church's recognition of the importance of the individual and of his or her abilities. Volunteers were not simply "cheap labor." Successful churches were also sensitive to the time constraints of volunteers, and considered the time they gave to ministry to be a precious, limited resource. The staff demonstrated true gratitude for the efforts of volunteers both by acknowledging their work and by working hand-in-hand with the laity in ministry.

Even beyond appreciation for their assistance, the full-time leaders of these churches possessed true respect for the laity. They rewarded volunteers with authentic respect for giving up their leisure time to be real servants of the Church.

"It's one thing for me to put in 8 or 10 hours a day on ministry," said one pastor. "I've been trained for this. I'm even paid for it. But think about what it means to work an eight-hour day in the marketplace, rush home to grab a dinner with the family, then run off to put in your remaining waking hours on ministry. They do it without pay," he went on, "sometimes without thanks, often without any real sense of reward for their effort. Now that's a heart for ministry. When I put in perspective what my people are doing to be part of this ministry, I can't help but be in awe of them. Frankly, sometimes their commitment embarrasses me into renewing my own efforts."

And yet, the pastor and staff did not fail to hold the laity accountable for the jobs they performed on behalf of the church. The experience of growing churches was that the volunteers wouldn't have had it any other way. Far from feeling threatened by accountability, these individuals were used to

Using volunteer services was not about merely assigning warm bodies to undone tasks. It was about enabling people to minister in the name of Christ by helping them to grow in their areas of giftedness.

performance demands, and had a greater respect for the church because they knew it would not accept a slipshod job.

GROWING IN GIFTEDNESS

Further, user friendly churches had a different perception of what service is all about. It was not merely assigning warm bodies to undone tasks. It was about enabling people to minister in the name of Christ by helping them to grow in their areas of giftedness, and to become more effective and capable servants of Christ. Unless the church challenged the individual to develop his or her abilities, chances were good that the individual would not grow. Just as muscles in our body only develop with exercise and training, so does lay leadership grow stronger with continued ministry guidance and experience.

"I still have trouble working through the whole volunteer ministry process," confessed one pastor, whose church counts several hundred people in lay ministries organized through the church. "My role is like that of a doctor. These people come to us because they know we have the goods to help them grow. They trust us. If I diagnose them wrong, there could be some severe side effects. In doing so, I have failed them. I have failed the church. These people are the single most important resource I have in my quest to reach the ministry goals I've identified."

Team Leadership

Because time is such an issue in the hectic lives of those who have leadership qualities, some successful churches experimented with a switch from solo leadership to team leadership strategies. Rather than overwhelm an individual with the entire mantle of responsibility for a given area of outreach, these churches searched for other compatible volunteers with leadership abilities to share the responsibility.

An important component of their outreach was that a representative of the church infrastructure—a pastor or staff member—shared the responsibility with them. This tactic not only sent a signal that the ministry is important, but helped the lay leaders to feel they were part of a true ministry team doing the work of the church.

Access to Resources

The church itself must also learn to operate as a resource bank. Few lay leaders have the time to reinvent the wheel when they are asked to do ministry. If there are existing resources—behavioral models, data bases, samples of teaching materials—it is more efficient for volunteer ministers to learn from them than to start from scratch and have to rely wholly upon their creative capabilities. In successful churches, identifying and warehousing such resources was an integral part of the staff's responsibilities. As the ministry teams were developed, some of the congregations even referred to the staff or pastoral person assigned to work with the team as the "resource person."

If the church wishes to build a good track record, it must remain sensitive to signs of volunteer burnout. Churches that fail to grow often fail to see burnout coming in volunteers, or else they see it coming and take it as a warning that they must squeeze every remaining ounce of life out of the volunteer before they collapse.

Volunteers in Training

User friendly churches, on the other hand, were more likely to anticipate burnout and have a training program in progress which provided a new squadron of leaders who could take up the slack while the people approaching burnout took time to renew their energies and excitement. People who had been serving for an extended period of time were often encouraged to take a break from programmed ministry, to recapture their energy before diving back in. Because the church was confident that people were being properly involved in ministry, and therefore were likely to feel fulfilled in their outreach efforts, they had little fear that the person would fail to return from their break.

One pastor, however, warned about letting people get too far away from the mainstream of ministry. "Sure, give them a period of renewal, a time for ministry convalescence. But don't take that concept too far. Remember, if you're doing what the Lord has called you to do, unless you're a maniac about it you're not likely to get to a point of ministry exhaustion. More often, in our church at least, the problem is that we allow people to take on too much responsibility. We can prevent a lot of the problems by monitoring what the folks are doing, and steering them clear of overcommitment."

The leader training process at growing churches was just one part of an ongoing effort to help people discover their gifts and use them for the benefit of the church. Again, a difference was evident between growing and stagnant churches. Growth-oriented churches had the attitude that it is the job of the church to prepare leaders to gain personal fulfillment through service to others. Stagnant churches were more likely to have the attitude that unless new leaders were trained to fill critical spots within the church's ministry, the church would suffer. Thus, the difference was in terms of who must benefit from the training. In the former case, the focus was upon the lay person's growth; in the latter case, it was upon the church's survival. The former is a situation of hope and encouragement. The latter is a situation of desperation and anxiety.

Finally, the healthy congregations not only counted upon the people to serve, but also demonstrated genuine delight in the ministry success of their laity. They meaningfully celebrated the involvement and the impact of their lay leaders. Rather than hand out the customary plaques and certificates for involvement, they provided them with reinforcement through relationships. Lay leaders had greater access to the staff and resources. They were celebrated in the midst of their peers (i.e.,

dinners, banquets, desserts). Because their impact was on people, they were recognized in front of people.

TAKING INVENTORY

Do people in your church volunteer once, but never return after
their term of service has expired? Perhaps they were burned
out. Perhaps they did not feel appreciated. Maybe they were
treated unprofessionally. It could be that they were asked to
do things that did not fit in their areas of giftedness. Do you
know what the problem was? You have a responsibility to find
out, and to respond appropriately. Recognize the signs of an
inefficient leadership placement and support program, and
make the necessary changes.

Has your church explored the meaning of spiritual gifts and
talents? If you were to ask the people of your church what their
areas of giftedness are, how many of them would be able to
confidently provide an answer? And how many of them understand the connection between their spiritual gifts and how they
devote their time and energy to the church? Consider the value
of consciously studying the relationship between gifts and outreach, and how every person in the church has special talents
that can be used to great effect.

Some churches believe they must change their volunteers to
make them more effective servants. Growing churches that
effectively use the laity in ministry, however, believe they must
identify the person's gifts and employ those gifts. They have
no interest in changing the person, only in refining his or her
raw gift. The church provides opportunities to be active in areas
of talent, rather than act as a school for correcting personal
deficiencies. Is your church more likely to accept people for who
they are and use their existing talents, or to identify ministry
possibilities and try to change the person into something they
are not?

Is your church a resource center for your leaders? Often,

churches fail to think of themselves as a bank of information and other resources from which leaders may make frequent withdrawals. Do you have staff who will assist volunteers in preparing lessons, understanding models of outreach, designing materials for use in different situations, or identifying other opportunities for reaching the community? Does your staff see this as part of their role, or are they simply relieved that there are lay people who will take some of the burden off their own shoulders?

What kind of training program do you offer to people? Is it long and drawn out, or is it intensive and stimulating? Don't make the mistake some churches make, treating adult volunteers as if they were brainless slaves. Take the time to know why these people want to be involved and are willing to sacrifice their time to do so. Capitalize on their desires and their talents, helping them to be what God has created and called them to be—not necessarily what your church was hoping they might be—toward filling the gaps.

SECTION IV TAKE OFF, PUT ON

But now you must rid yourselves of all such things as these:...since you have taken off your old self with its practices and have put on the new self, which is being renewed in knowledge in the image of its Creator....Therefore, as God's chosen people, holy and dearly loved, clothe yourselves with compassion, kindness, humility, gentleness and patience (Col. 3:8-10,12).

CHURCH GROWTH CAN BE DESCRIBED AS TAKING OFF OF the Body of Christ all outmoded or ineffective garments, and clothing it instead with garments that identify it as the attractive Bride of Christ. This section gathers insights about growing churches in the form of what those surveyed for this report "put off"—what they did *not* do. It also includes answers to questions that are most often asked by those who are interested in adapting proven methods to their own situation.

Naturally, it is most common to describe a dynamic, growing church in terms of the things it does that are most responsible for its success. However, many activities or perspectives that growing churches did *not* have are just as critical to understanding their nature and progress.

In some instances, growing churches challenged the prevailing notion of what a church must do in order to be a church. They did not automatically buy into an assumption of what ministry "must" look like, or what procedures "must" be in place to legitimize a ministry. In other instances, growing congregations consciously rejected common conventions in favor of developing a more comfortable or more meaningful approach to a specific aspect of ministry. They did not dismiss the importance of that aspect of outreach. Instead, they believed the same ministry could better be accomplished through a different approach.

Putting on and taking off...consider these ministry "garments" in the light of your own situation. ➡

16 WHAT USER FRIENDLY CHURCHES DID *NOT* DO

The healthy churches in this study were not characterized by copying other churches. Here are 10 programs, perceptions and behaviors commonly found in Protestant churches in America *but conspicuous by their absence* in most of the user friendly churches surveyed for this book.

SUCCESSFUL CHURCHES DID NOT LIMIT GOD

Stagnant and declining churches frequently restrict the scope of their ministry because they doubt that God would bless unusual or enormous efforts. They do not boldly proclaim "We won't do it because God can't handle it," of course, but the fear that underlies their reticence is paramount to such a proclamation. They assume the role of "God's protector," keeping Him from failing and thereby losing the respect of, and impact upon, the masses.

Growing churches had an intense, unshakable belief that God is capable of accomplishing anything. When their church accepted a ministry direction, it was based upon prayer, Bible study and the discernment and wisdom of godly people. They pursued the ministry direction with the earnest belief that they had been called to that ministry by God, and therefore fully expected Him to bless their efforts. They believed that the ministry would be blessed in His timing, in His way. On occasion, they engaged in an area of ministry whose viability seemed uncertain, but they threw themselves into it wholeheartedly because they believed that God had called them to it. In those instances, especially, they trusted God to bless their efforts, for reasons and purposes that they may not have understood.

THEY DIDN'T BEAT A DEAD HORSE

Churches that struggle often seek to maintain programs that are failing, believing that sufficient tinkering will breathe life into those programs. They fear that acknowledging that a program has failed will signal to the people that the church is incapable of effective ministry, or that the leaders are not effective leaders.

Alternatively, failing churches often make the mistake of returning to the well once too often. Desperate to find a theme or strategy that strikes a responsive chord, they rely upon that approach in each new ministry effort, leaving the people with a tarnished memory of what could have been a good and successful outreach. There are countless examples: the concert series that no longer attracts people, the campy church theatrical productions that have long since ceased to be fresh and funny, the forced messages about political issues that have no real audience, the advertising campaigns that continue to play off of outdated jokes or characterizations, etc.

Even the growing churches made mistakes. Sometimes their errors were minor and inconsequential; at other times, they were large and significant. However, successful churches were quick to recognize their errors, and to acknowledged that they "blew it." They were willing to remove weak or failing programs. And they were willing to interrupt a successful program after it peaked, leaving the people satisfied and wanting more, rather than trying to squeeze every last ounce of impact out of a program, risking overkill and boredom.

SUCCESSFUL CHURCHES DID NOT HUMILIATE VISITORS

In many stagnant churches, anonymity is next to ungodliness. The underlying assumption is that friendliness and Christian love can only be shown by showering attention on the visitor. The effort is meant to make the person feel welcome and special. Exit interviews, however, indicate that such attention is generally undesired and often causes the visitor to feel violated. In their desire to embrace the newcomer, these churches unwittingly trample the line between a warm welcome and overwhelming, uncomfortable pressure.

Anonymity for visitors was not perceived to be negative by the leaders of growing churches. They recognized that many people visit a church with trepidation, and with a desire to take things slowly. These cautious visitors often prefer to remain part of the woodwork for awhile, acting as participant-observers, unobtrusive and unfettered. The leaders of these churches also believed that the members of the congregation could be relied upon to do what was reasonable and necessary to make the visitor feel welcomed, but not cornered.

THEY WERE NOT INSULATED FROM THE COMMUNITY

A church that is struggling for existence is more inclined either to attempt to bully neighbors to accept its sociopolitical stands, or more likely, to hibernate and become uninvolved in the affairs of the community. This is one of the outgrowths of the inward focus of the church. It is endemic to churches that have little understanding of how to touch the lives of people within their realm of need. While none of the successful churches was a political power broker, all had established a sensitive and significant presence in the broader activity of the community. Struggling churches tended to retreat from any community responsibility, indicating that they were having enough trouble making the church programs functional, without diluting their resources through community involvement.

The pastors of successful churches spent substantial amounts of time with community leaders and at non-church functions. The congregation perceived the church as a part of the community, not apart from the community. The concept of being salt in the world was translated to mean that the church must do whatever it could to be available when the community needed help, to be present when key decisions were being made, and to be willing to shoulder its portion of the responsibility for making the community one which included spirituality in its inherent fabric.

THEY DID NOT ALIENATE THOSE WHO ARE DIFFERENT

Dying churches frequently allow their own insecurities to preclude the acceptance of people whose viewpoints or actions challenge what the church stands for. Rather than accept the person and reject their behavior, they are likely to reject both, as if they were inseparable. This inevitably creates a chasm between the person and the church that is both difficult and unlikely to be bridged.

A healthy church is one that is confident in its beliefs, secure in the love of the God it serves and certain that part of its reason for existence is to reach those people whose relationship with God is weak, insignificant or nonexistent. In the process of trying to understand and impact those people, the church remains firm in its doctrine, but not abusive or abrasive. It recognizes the difference between rejecting ideas and rejecting the people who hold those ideas. Jesus rejected ideas and behav-

Struggling churches tended to retreat from community responsibility, indicating that they were having enough trouble making the church programs functional, without diluting their resources through community involvement.

iors that conflicted with God's law; but He never admonished His followers to reject the *people* who manifest such thoughts, words or deeds. Instead, He called them to remain in close contact with those people, sharing over and over, in new and relevant ways, the Christian perspective.

NO COLD-CALL EVANGELISM

Falling into the familiar patterns and routines that have worked in the past is a trademark of stagnant churches. Cold-call evangelism is one such pattern that appeals to many such churches.

During the first three-quarters of this century, it was not uncommon for churches to develop evangelistic teams that would get together one or two nights a week, and go knocking on people's doors, attempting to share the gospel on people's front door steps, or in their living rooms.

Times have changed, however, and successful churches grow because they have generally understood the change. They may have an evangelism team, but the efforts of that team are directed either to "response evangelism"—visiting those people who request such a visit, or "event evangelism"—providing public interest events that include some type of evangelistic thrust. They know that the chances of meeting a responsive individual who gets a cold call at their front door are minimal. They know that their good-hearted attempt at service may close the person's mind to the gospel. Given the range of other, proven means of affecting change in the person's heart, they simply do not believe that the methodology warrants the high risk of failure.

THEY DID NOT APOLOGIZE FOR SEEKING HELP

Stagnant churches frequently lack the resources to grow because they do not provide people with a compelling reason to give, do not express the appropriate gratitude for that which is given and are embarrassed to ask for what they really need. Sometimes they set their sights too low. Thus, even when their demands are met, they have failed.

It takes time, money, equipment, space and effort to make a church successful. At growing churches, this was a recognized reality. Leaders believed that everybody likes to be affiliated with a winner, and they did not hesitate to ask people to get involved or to sacrifice some of their resources for the good of the Body. Nor were they apologetic in their requests. They were sensitive to the hardships created by personal sacrifice, but provided as accurate and compelling a case as possible in describing their needs. Just as important, they were quick and genuine in expressing their thanks to those who offered what was needed to make the ministry solvent and progressive.

THEY DID NOT AVOID CONFRONTATION

The leaders of stagnant churches rarely have a direct confrontation with people whose behavior or attitudes are both wrong and detrimental to the health of the Body. Sometimes, this is because the personality of the church leader is non-confrontational. In other cases, it is because the dominant desire of church leaders is to keep people coming to the church; confrontation, they reason, might diminish the Body. In all cases, the refusal to confront that which is wrong or harmful is one manifestation of the inability of the church to model the principles that make the Scriptures so invaluable in a sinful world.

User friendly churches encountered their fair share of situations in which people needed to be confronted. These churches did not interpret "love" to mean "step all over me if you must, but because I am a Christian I will accept that abuse." Instead, they took the "tough love" perspective: there is a distinction between right and wrong, and I will love you regardless, but I will also let you know when you are in the wrong. The confrontation had to be done delicately, and in accordance with the guidelines provided in Scripture; but sin is not to be tolerated under any circumstances.

STAFFING NOT BASED ON PRECEDENT

Many churches seem to hire staff according to what the typical church would do—first the senior pastor, next the music director, then the education director, etc.

Stagnant churches generally do not have to worry about adding new positions; their primary need is often to fill vacated positions. However, the tendency is generally to bring in a person to provide the same type of ministry expertise that was recently vacated, instead of identifying what type of resource person would best meet the potential of the church.

This was not so at growing churches. Their personnel decisions tended to be need-driven. If their ministry was growing in adult singles' ministry, a person who specialized in singles' ministry was the next addition, regardless of how organizationally lopsided or unusual the staff looked to an outsider. These churches did not believe that there is a standard progression for hiring. They hired the staff they needed, and they got the best available candidate to fill the slot.

THEY DIDN'T TAKE THE SAFE ROUTE

Stagnant churches are often secure with the status quo. Risks are viewed as the opportunity to fail, rather than the chance to experience a breakthrough. They are more likely to accept the usual than the creative. They are more likely to continue the routine than to try the unique. They prefer the comfort of stability to the discomfort of growth.

Growing churches got to where they were because they were willing to take measured risks. They were willing to do some unusual things, to demonstrate creativity in their approach to reaching people. They generally understood that to be safe in ministry is to be stifled. To make gains, a church must take some risks.

17 CAN *YOUR* CHURCH GROW?

INDISPUTABLY, SOME CHURCHES IN AMERICA ARE GROWING QUICK-ly. They have developed a holistic, effective ministry that is the envy of pastors and lay leaders for miles around. Through the outreach of those churches, lives are being changed and the kingdom of God is growing.

But the question you're probably asking yourself is: "Can I do the same thing with my church?"

Since writing the report on which this book is based, and conducting church growth seminars around the nation, three related questions have popped up over and over again. In closing, let's address those questions.

CAN ANY CHURCH GROW?

Sure, the churches studied for this book made it happen. But what about the small, denominational church in Ames, Iowa, that hasn't seen the attendance meter jump more than a hair in either direction in over 20 years? What about the store-front mission church in downtown Philadelphia that struggles to pay the rent, much less tap into the high tech, high cost resources that make the megachurches so glamorous and attractive? What about the 600-member mainline, liturgical church in the affluent suburb that doesn't seem to have much life in its services, its programs or the spiritual demeanor of the congregation? Is it even possible for these churches to grow?

I believe it is—under certain conditions. My perception of the growing churches was that they were on a mission. They knew who they were, where they were headed, how they planned to get there and why it was vital for them to do so. They had a sense of the likely obstacles, and how they planned to respond. They were leaving as little to chance as possible. They understood that building an authentic church was going to require a tremendous amount of capital—human capital as well as financial. Growth was not an accessory to their ministry. It was a central indication of whether or not they had a ministry.

Key Elements of the Growth Equation

These churches had certain qualities that were indispensable to growth. As we have noted, without a strong leadership team, comprised of both pastoral and lay leaders, growth would have remained a dream. Without a united vision of God's mission for the congregation, it would not have been possible to make headway. Unless the individuals who were the church were sincerely committed to growing the church, it would not have happened.

The commitment could not end with intellectual assent that "growth is good." The congregation had to prove their commitment by laboring long hours, sacrificing personal resources and engaging in serious prayer and study related to the health of the church. Lacking a comprehensive plan or strategy for expansion, the odds of the pieces falling together were slim to none. And unless the attitude of the congregation

Growth is not...based on a static, one-time self-discovery....It must be viewed as evolutionary. Growing churches are committed to discovering and resdiscovering the subtleties...of their environment and reacting to that information within the context of ministry.

reflected a heart turned over to God, the entire process would be a charade.

Mission Possible
Any church that can pull these elements together can certainly support growth. But as you know if you've tried to do this, it's not as easy as it may sound.

Growth is not an overnight process. Neither is it based upon a static, one-time self-discovery. The needs of the target population and the abilities and resources within the congregation are fluid. Thus, the plan and associated activities resulting in real growth for the church must be viewed as evolutionary. Growing churches are committed to discovering and rediscovering the subtleties and nuances of their environment, and reacting to that information within the context of their call to ministry. They take care to nurture the existing body during this critical incubation period, without losing sight of the longer-term goals.

I've also come to believe that it is substantially easier to achieve growth in a church that has been newly planted than in an existing congregation that is beset with hardening of the spiritual arteries. In a new church, the chances of bringing together people of like mind and like mission are much greater. In such churches, attracting people who own the common vision for ministry is much more probable. Indeed, it takes such a oneness of mind and spirit to successfully launch a church in America today.

For the church that has a long history and has been stuck on an attendance plateau for some time, or perhaps has been slowly deteriorating, turnaround is a major challenge. You're fighting preconceived notions of what the church is meant to be, based upon historical precedent. You're faced with individuals who are faithful members, but who may not have the zeal, the energy, the vision or the interest to birth a renewal process. The existing image of the church, the appearance and condition of the facilities, the attitude of the pastor and staff toward what they are and are not willing to change—all these things and more may block the road to growth.

Can it be done? Yes, but it takes an extraordinary leader guiding a special group of disciples to create the will and the means. Don't sell the challenge short: if you're going to go for it, you've got to put everything you've got on the line, and take a no-holds-barred approach.

IS AN EXTRAORDINARY PASTOR ESSENTIAL?

There is no mistake about it: the pastors of these churches are extraordinary men of God. They are leading superb churches into areas that other churches wouldn't dare consider. Without an incredibly gifted leader, these churches probably would not have made the noteworthy gains that brought them to my attention.

And yet, some of these individuals were not viewed as extraordinary when they first came to their current churches. Some of them had tried to plant churches, and failed. Some of them were midlevel staff people of no particular distinction who were hired by their current church because they exhibited some raw, untested talent. A few of them took time to gain their footing before catching a second wind and setting the congregation on fire. In short, I do not believe these individuals were bound to succeed, but that they were determined to grow to the levels of achievement demanded by the current situation.

Without exception, each of these men lives from day to day for a single purpose: to bring honor and glory to God through whatever service they are capable of performing. The single-minded devotion they exhibit is unmistakable. If this makes a person extraordinary, then yes, a church is likely to grow only if it is led by an extraordinary pastor.

Some of these pastors laugh about their initial efforts at being a persuasive preacher. But nobody laughs at them now. They have diligently sought to improve their communication skills. Some took speech lessons. Others listened to tapes of leading preachers and tried to emulate them. A few enrolled in post-graduate programs to enhance their speaking abilities. All of them sought the constructive criticism of a few respected individuals, and responded to that advice. If becoming a gifted speaker who has persistently worked at refining that gift is the mark of an extraordinary pastor, then yes, a church is likely to grow only if it is led by an extraordinary pastor.

In every case I studied, the church was more than the sum of the efforts of the senior pastor. The church was growing because the pastor had helped people catch the vision, gain necessary training, have ample opportunities for personal ministry and feel good about their involvement in the work of the Church. The pastor was just as likely to gain satisfaction from watching the flock minister as from his own ministry. If this behavior and attitude is what constitutes an extraordinary pastor, then yes, a church is likely to grow only if it is led by an extraordinary pastor.

DO *ALL* THESE PRINCIPLES HAVE TO BE ADOPTED?

As mentioned earlier, it is important *not* to seek to grow by copying every move made by these churches. Your community, your congregation, the resources you have, the gifts of the people who are doing the ministry—are factors that vary from church to church, requiring a customized approach to growing the church.

However, I would also caution that what enabled these churches to grow had more to do with *their responsiveness to their environment* than with specific programs and structures. The factor underlying the success they realized had more to do with their holistic, comprehensive perspective about the church and how to encompass people within that ministry, than with a series of techniques or methods.

The danger of utilizing a bits-'n'-pieces patchwork strategy for growth is that certain elements may prove to be incompatible with each other. You don't need to buy the game plan of the churches reviewed in this book lock, stock and barrel. But whatever you decide to do, make sure that you have a well-rounded, full-blown plan based on a workable understanding of people, spiritual growth and church dynamics.

GETTING ON WITH IT

America represents one of the great untapped mission fields in the world today. Isn't it interesting that North America represents the one continent on which Christianity is not growing? Throughout the world, however, the Church is blossoming as never before. We, too, should join in that growth trend.

The time is ripe for new models of ministry to be tried, tested, refined and disseminated. The time is ripe for a new generation of church leaders to emerge, anxious to lead the Church into an age of growth and impact.

Nothing worth winning is won easily, of course. Even the most gifted and blessed of leaders have pursued their vision against considerable odds and barriers. This is a biblical standard, starting with Moses and continuing through the lives of some of God's most favored servants (Joshua, David, Solomon, Paul, Peter). The pastors of the healthy churches reviewed in this book are quick to admit that the joys of growth were not without trials. "Tell them that they can do it if they're willing to fail, and willing to give it everything they've got," warned one pastor about the enormous effort required for growing a church. "It's never as easy as it looks from the outside, but it's a lot more satisfying than you'd expect."

Pray for the Church. Pray about your role in the growth of the Body and the support of those who have been specially gifted to lead the Church into the 21st century.

And let's get on with it

THIS BOOK IS AN OUTGROWTH OF THE WORK OF THE BARNA Research Group. The company seeks to provide Christian ministries with current, accurate and actionable information that will enable Christian ministries to be more effective. In addition to conducting customized research for individual ministries, Barna Research provides the following ministry resources:

- a quarterly newsletter *(Ministry Currents)* on societal conditions and trends, and their relationship to the Church;
- research-based reports on specific ministry issues. These reports include studies of how to reach the unchurched, ministry to teenagers, single adults and the Church, church growth strategies, sources of information on conditions affecting ministry, life-styles of born again Christians, and more;
- in-person presentations by George Barna and Barna Research staff, designed to address the needs and interests of conference and seminar registrants;
- other ministry resources (audiotapes, videotapes).

**For further information about the
Barna Research Group, please write to them at
P.O. Box 4152, Glendale, CA 91222-0152.**